Following
MUHAMMAD

ISLAMIC CIVILIZATION & MUSLIM NETWORKS

Carl W. Ernst and Bruce B. Lawrence, editors

Following MUHAMMAD

Rethinking Islam in the

Contemporary World

CARL W. ERNST

The University of North Carolina Press

Chapel Hill & London

This book was published with the assistance of the
William R. Kenan Jr. Fund of the University of North Carolina Press.

Frontispiece:

Illustration of Mecca from *Dala'il al-Khayrat* of al-Jazuli
(The Ackland Art Museum, University of North Carolina at Chapel Hill,
Ackland Fund, selected by The Ackland Associates)

Library of Congress Cataloging-in-Publication Data

Ernst, Carl W., 1950–

Following Muhammad: rethinking Islam in the contemporary world /
Carl W. Ernst.

p. cm. — (Islamic civilization and Muslim networks)

Includes bibliographical references and index.

ISBN 0-8078-2837-8 (cloth: alk. paper)

1. Islam — 21st century. 2. Islam — Essence, genius, nature.

I. Title. II. Series.

BP161.3 .E76   2003

303.48'21767101821 — dc21   2003011162

07 06 05 04 03   5 4 3 2 1

To my students,

past and present,

and to the memory of my teacher,

Annemarie Schimmel

لاُستاذتى آن ماری شمل

رحمهاالله

CONTENTS

ILLUSTRATIONS

PREFACE

What images are conjured today by the word "Islam"? Walk into any bookstore, and you will initially be drawn to a stack of breathless titles that are truly frightening. These journalistic exposés reveal worlds of terrorist intrigue and plots against the United States. Alongside these instant potboilers are books with a more sober tone, delivering with masterful condescension the verdict of failure upon Islamic civilization, and the promise of an apocalyptic clash between Islam and the West. Tucked into a corner one may find a few academic surveys of Islamic theology and history, written in the tedious and excruciating prose reserved for textbooks. There may also be a couple of apologetics written by Muslims, attempting to defend Islam against any accusations. Finally, and most impenetrable of all, there will be two or three translations of the Qur'an, a foreign text that remains an enigmatic and unreadable cipher. How can anyone make sense of all this?

This book has been written to provide a completely different alternative to currently available books on Islam. What is offered here is a sympathetic yet reasoned and analytical view of the Islamic religious tradition and the contemporary issues that Muslims face. My most radical departure from conventional wisdom is to propose a nonfundamentalist understanding of Islam.

Both the difficulty and the importance of this task are illustrated by two events that took place in 2002. First, it was in the summer of that year that I delivered the completed manuscript of this book to the publisher who had initially commissioned it.

To my complete astonishment, after considerable delay, the publisher informed me that the press would not be able to publish the book. There was no question regarding the quality of the manuscript; this was, instead, a matter of personal attitudes among the editorial staff, resulting from the terrorist attacks against American targets on September 11, 2001. I was told that some of the editors were now personally uncomfortable with being associated with any book on a subject that could be used to justify terrorism. The identity of the publisher is unimportant. What is most remarkable about this incident is that it demonstrates the extent to which, even in the world of publishing, the subject of Islam has become so controversial that some people cannot confront it.

The second example was the Summer Reading Program at the University of North Carolina at Chapel Hill (UNC), where I teach. Ordinarily this kind of assignment attracts little attention, except as an unwelcome intrusion on students' vacation time. This year, however, the committee in charge of the selection wanted to choose a book that would address some of the issues raised by the September 11 attacks. Having discarded several weighty tomes on Middle Eastern history, terrorism, and similar topics, they asked me whether it would be advisable to assign our first-year students to read a translation of the Qur'an. I enthusiastically recommended Michael Sells's *Approaching the Qur'an: The Early Revelations*, a brilliant multimedia translation that is ideal for introducing this challenging text. While Sells's book was not designed to explain the mentalities of terrorists, it did offer our students a first encounter with one of the most influential books in world history. This assignment attracted national and international attention, as a conservative Virginia-based Christian group sued UNC, arguing that we were infringing on students' religious freedom by trying to convert them to Islam. Members of the North Carolina state legislature reacted with fury to this assignment, seeing it as equivalent to support for Muslim terrorists. Although federal courts dismissed the lawsuit, so that more than 2,000 students proceeded to discuss the book without incident, the outrage over the university assigning a book about Islam revealed once again a deep-seated fear and hostility that opposed even reading a book on the subject.

Under these circumstances—when publishers, religious groups, and politicians are opposed to an impartial and fair-minded discussion of Islam—it is painfully obvious that such a discussion is exactly what we need. The modern debate about Islam in America and Europe has been conducted primarily through sensational journalism and ideological attack. Although excellent scholarship on Islam is available, it is all too often couched in impenetrable prose and buried in obscure academic journals. *Following Muhammad* is designed to cut through the fog of suspicion and misinformation; it offers readers the tools to reach an independent understanding of key themes and historical settings affecting Muslims—and non-Muslims—around the world today.

This book is the result of many years of thinking, teaching, and writing about Islamic religion and culture. I was initially drawn to Islamic studies by my personal encounter with the Persian poetry of great Sufis (Muslim mystics) such as Jalal al-Din Rumi. Precisely because of widespread ignorance and misunderstanding of Islam, it occurred to me that the study of the great spiritual and humanistic tradition of Sufism, as a major aspect of Islamic thought and practice, would be an appropriate way to bridge the civilizational gap. I still think this is a good idea; years later, much to my amazement, I have observed the remarkable popularity that Rumi has attained in America, thanks to poets and translators such as Coleman Barks and Robert Bly.

In the process of my education, I learned Arabic, Persian, and Urdu and got a Ph.D. in Islamic studies. I spent time overseas, primarily in Eastern, non-Arab countries, particularly India and Pakistan, with research visits to Iran and Turkey.

Like everyone else in the small group of American scholars who work on the study of Islam, I have found my humanistic goals running afoul of political events again and again. I had air reservations to go to Tehran for dissertation research in the fall of 1978, but the Iranian revolution forced me to switch to India instead. In 1985 I had a Fulbright Islamic Civilization Research grant to study in India, but someone in the Indian government thought that my research on medieval Sufis was too controversial to permit a visa; consequently, my family and I spent a wonderful year in Pakistan. For a change, I had just finished my research in Istanbul when Iraq invaded Kuwait in 1990. In the fall of 1998, though, I was forced to postpone a research trip to Pakistan when the U.S. government fired cruise missiles into Sudan and Afghanistan in retaliation for embassy bombings in East Africa. And I began to write these lines in the wonderful city of Seville, once a center of the Moorish culture of medieval Spain, in the shadow of the terrorist attacks of September 11, 2001.

The educational task faced by specialists in Islamic studies is enormous. There exists, on one hand, a tremendous ignorance and suspicion about Islam in much of Europe and America, now considerably enhanced by recent tragedy. On the other hand, there are extremists from Muslim countries who have used the language of Islam to justify horrific acts of mass violence. Lost in this confrontation are hundreds of millions of Muslims who inhabit the world today who have been classified as outsiders to Western civilization but who do not share the apocalyptic and fanatic vision of an Osama bin Ladin. Those of us who have studied the text of the Qur'an, the writings of the great poets, and the history of Islamic civilization feel very keenly the distortion and perversion of Islamic symbols and authority perpetrated by these modern extremists. How much more anguish is felt by the vast majority of Muslims, who loathe acts of terrorism at the same time that they deeply resent the continued imposition of neocolonial influence over their countries?

Despite these extraordinary challenges, the task of Islamic studies could also be described as minimal. In 1992 I participated in a workshop discussing images of Islam in America. The educational goal that we finally settled on in the workshop was very basic: to convince Americans that Muslims are human beings. This might sound like an absurdly simple point, but the Islamic religion is perhaps the one remaining subject about which educated people are content to demonstrate outright prejudice and bias. Ten years later a workshop on critical issues in Islamic studies came to the same conclusion, but more forcefully: the real issue is to humanize Muslims in the eyes of non-Muslims. I will discuss the nature of anti-Islamic prejudice in detail in Chapter 1, but it still amazes me that intelligent people can believe that all Muslims are violent or that all Muslim women are oppressed, when they would never dream of uttering slurs stereotyping much smaller groups such as Jews or blacks. The strength of these negative images of Muslims is remarkable, even though they are not based on personal experience or actual study, but they receive daily reinforcement from the news media and popular culture.

The arguments presented in this book are designed to bring the reader into a new relationship with the subject of Islam by providing critical and independent access to key information. In my previous books, I have developed a method of explaining unfamiliar religious subjects that avoids the jargon of specialized scholarship. I believe it is possible to write clearly and directly and to engage the reader in the subject, not by authoritarian pronouncements, but by clarifying the debates and showing what is at stake. I draw particularly on religious studies and on historical context to bring out detailed meanings and comparisons. Approaching the subject from religious studies, I draw attention to the important role of modern Christianity, particularly Protestant thought, in shaping modern interpretations of Islam. These interpretations are found in the writings of non-Muslim European and American experts on Islam (the so-called Orientalists), and they also occur in works by modern Muslim authors and critics. By paying attention to historical context, I bring out the political, economic, and social factors behind phenomena sometimes thought to be exclusively religious.

Using these methods, I initially planned for the book to revolve around major Islamic religious themes, with an emphasis on the little-understood role of the Prophet Muhammad as the central figure defining Islamic religiosity. That still remains the basic underpinning of this book. The aftermath of the terrorist attacks of September 11, however, has created an environment in which we can no longer afford to neglect the problem of religious and civilizational confrontation mentioned above; for many people, confrontation is the only way they have ever heard Islam described. The main difference this has made for the book has been to highlight how we have constructed the notion of religion in recent history around the ideas of competition and confrontation, since all too often this modern world–imperial concept of religion is allowed to pass unexamined.

It is particularly important to clarify the interplay between religion and history, because the culture of mass media today tends to create the notion that the present is the only time worth considering. The flood of advertisements and entertainment that we all endure on a daily basis encourages amnesia about the past and reinforces contemporary ideologies as if they were eternal. Knowledge of the past, however, can be an important tool for liberating oneself from the tyranny of the current climate of opinion. Words and concepts do not simply grow on trees; they have been invented for specific purposes, and the history of their changing use reveals the crucial issues that define our world. Knowing the origins and transformations of words allows us to decide which of their implications we wish to endorse, and which of our predecessors' objectives we can still subscribe to. Approaching religion from the perspective of history also reveals that behind the apparently seamless unity of religious concepts lie major debates and differences, signs of irrevocable pluralism, and multiple perspectives within every religious tradition. Although it is tempting to listen to voices that claim undisputed authority pronouncing blanket approvals or condemnations on all kinds of subjects, that seduction is open to charges of prejudice and bias. I invite the reader to take on instead the excitement of discovering how rich and varied the changing history of a religion such as Islam has actually been.

This book is not meant to be an apologetic defense of Islam against criticisms; I myself am not a Muslim, and I am not offering preferential treatment to anyone. This book does offer the thesis that Muslims are human beings — meaning that they have history and that they live in multiple social and historical situations defined by economic class, ethnicity, gender, and all the factors that ordinary human beings have to deal with. On a very basic level, I feel personally compelled to make this minimal argument because of the profoundly human relationships I have established with Muslims over the years, with people who have invited me into their homes and welcomed me into their families. Although years ago I originally envisioned my professional task as educating non-Muslims about a foreign culture, the growing presence of Muslims in America and Europe has created a new constituency urgently committed to thinking through what it means to be a Muslim today. Muslims constitute nearly one-fourth of the human race, and that proportion is not likely to change; so it is simply a fact that non-Muslims need to come to terms with Islam as a part of our common humanity. It is also a fact that Muslims who are not satisfied with authoritative pronouncements will need to come to terms both with the history of their predecessors and with the history of the modern world. This book is written for both these audiences rather than for scholars, and it aims to be illustrative and provocative rather than comprehensive or exhaustive.

The basic method of this book is therefore descriptive and interpretive. It intends to provide the reader with the key concepts and questions necessary to understand contemporary debates about Islam. I do not wish to privilege any particular position, but an approach based on religious studies and historical context is bound to give a critical treatment to the issues. That is, as explained above, religious claims are not accepted at face value, and appeals to authority are not allowed to trump rational argument or to ignore history. Instead, everything is evaluated in terms of the elements of historical context that can be discussed by anyone, Muslim or non-Muslim, regardless of background or precommitments.

To make the book more accessible, I have written it in the form of an essay, only lightly burdened by notes except to give due credit or pointers to additional sources, including materials available on the Internet. As I have discovered in the past few years, Internet sources increasingly provide access to an astonishing range of materials relating to Islam that were previously almost impossible for the average reader to find. For the convenience of readers, I have set up a website (‹http://www.unc.edu/~cernst/islam.htm›) containing all the Internet references in this book, which will be regularly updated and expanded in an attempt to keep up with the growth of these resources. Contributions and suggestions from readers will be welcome.

While this book aims primarily to reveal the human face of

Islam, it can only do so by removing the veils of ignorance that have cloaked this subject for centuries in the minds of Europeans and Americans. Restoration of anything like an honest picture involves two kinds of mental operations: one is the complication of the cartoonlike stereotypes that dominate our current perceptions, giving Muslims a full three-dimensional human complexity; the other is the revival of memory, to replace the selective amnesia that has blotted out subjects such as colonialism from our common memory even of the recent past. The method that I use is to provide real human examples, which require the reader to construct a narrative that will help to explain how such things have come to be. In this way the reader participates in the creative act of reimagining as human an immense group of people who have been demonized. The reader should not feel, however, that he or she is being blamed for the prejudices that we have inherited. Some audiences to whom I have presented this analysis have reacted with surprise, frequently commenting that they had absolutely no concept of Islam whatever, that it was a great big blank in their minds. While acknowledging the truth of these reactions, I still wish to point out the surprising ways in which the dominant self-conception of Euro-Americans is in conflict with the actual history of our predecessors' engagement with Islam. Restoring a human face to Islam also means coming to a better knowledge of who we all are.

One final admission is necessary: I hate textbooks. I have attempted over the past twenty years to avoid using regular textbooks in my classes in religious studies because they generally offer students the deceptive appearance of easy and authoritative conclusions about the subject. Religion is a very complex topic, though, and I would much rather have students experience creative doubt and questioning than have them memorize a simple answer in the hope of passing an exam. I have been particularly dissatisfied with textbooks on Islam, beginning with

H. A. R. Gibb's unfortunately titled *Mohammedanism* (first published in 1947 and still in print; in subsequent editions, the name was finally changed to *Islam*). Although that book was in some ways a masterful summary, it set the pattern for subsequent textbooks on Islam by adopting a subject division taken from the scholastic curriculum of medieval Sunni Muslim theologians. To this outline, mirroring the classical bias of Orientalist scholarship, it added a brief supplementary chapter on contemporary Islamic history. The main variation on this pattern has been to give weight to certain contemporary reformist and fundamentalist interpretations of Islam, in effect recognizing them as the authoritative mainstream.

What I offer here instead is an interpretive essay that attempts to view Islamic religious history as a source of the contemporary situation, with attention to major debates that frame a broad range of religious expression and opinion. At the same time, I wish to highlight the impact of Euro-American attitudes on Muslims in the colonial and postcolonial eras. This book has been written, in short, to stimulate communication between Muslims and non-Muslims in the world they have commonly inherited.

The first chapter of the book presents an overview of Islam as part of the modern world for at least the past two centuries, including anti-Islamic attitudes from medieval times to the present. Chapter 2 considers the history of the term "religion" and how it changed from the time of early Christianity to the early colonial era. This permits a fresh consideration of how Islam is understood by scholars, how it is defined by the nation-state and by government bureaucrats, and how Muslims have conceptualized it in their own terms.

Chapter 3, "The Sacred Sources of Islam," begins with the life of the Prophet Muhammad and proceeds to an overview of the Qur'an, its structure, and its contents. Without attempting to cover every fact or detail, this interpretation emphasizes the central role of the Prophet Muhammad for Islamic religious consciousness. This chapter also provides the opportunity to reconsider the major international debates that have raged over the Qur'an in recent fictional and journalistic writing. Chapter 4, "Ethics and Life in the World," begins with the broad concept of Islamic religious ethics deriving from both authoritative texts and philosophical inquiry. After demonstrating the major role of Greek philosophical ethics in Islamic thought, it moves on to the changes in ethical thinking during the period of European colonial domination. A series of major problems for religious ethics then follows, including the concept of an Islamic state, liberal Islamic thought, gender issues and the question of veiling, and the relationship between Islam and science.

Chapter 5, "Spirituality in Practice," investigates spirituality and mysticism in the traditions of Sufism and Shi'ism, with particular attention to the role of Sufi saints and Shi'i Imams as spiritual guides and mediators; controversies such as the Wahhabi rejection of sainthood also come in for discussion. This chapter also asks about the nature of Islamic art, including sacred art, secular art with religious themes, Islamic art for non-Muslims, and the significance of fantasies of Muslim cultures in European Orientalist painting. The book concludes with "Reimagining Islam in the Twenty-first Century," a look at how ideology and technology are continually transforming the way that Muslims and non-Muslims imagine this religious tradition. Throughout, the book underlines the role of the Prophet Muhammad as the chief defining figure for the distinctiveness of Islamic experience.

Writing this book would not have been possible without the continuous interaction I have had with students in classes on Islamic studies at every level over the past twenty years; it is in part to them that I dedicate this book, as those entrusted with the task of improving our knowledge of these subjects in the future. I particularly would like to acknowledge the students in two first-year seminars on Islam at the University of North Carolina at Chapel Hill, plus graduate student assistants Philip Hassett, Karen Ruffle, and Peter Wright, all of whom helped me work through many of the topics discussed in this book in 2000–2002.

I owe particular thanks to Elaine Maisner and the staff of the University of North Carolina Press, who had the vision to see this book as a contribution both to the academy and to public debate. It is also of considerable personal significance to me that UNC Press published in 1975 one of the most important books ever produced in America in the area of Islamic studies, *Mystical Dimensions of Islam*, by my former teacher, the late Annemarie Schimmel (d. 2003). This book is also dedicated to her, and I am sorry that she did not live to see it.

I would in addition like to thank my colleagues in the field of Islamic studies and related subjects, who have continually challenged me and helped me to come to new insights as we have grappled with this topic over the years. Special thanks go to the people I work with most closely here in North Carolina, at UNC (Edward Curtis, Bart Ehrman, Charles Kurzman, James Peacock, Shantanu Phukan, Sarah Shields, and Thomas Tweed), Duke University (miriam cooke, Katherine Ewing, Bruce Lawrence, and Ebrahim Moosa), and North Carolina State University (David Gilmartin, Akram Khater, and Tony Stewart), and also to Richard Martin (Emory University), Brannon Wheeler (University of Washington), Muhammad Qasim Zaman (Brown University), F. Canguzel Zulfikar, and Tahir Andrabi (Pomona College). Several anonymous reviewers of this manuscript, plus Michael Sells (Haverford College) and Frances Robinson (Royal Holloway, University of London), made valuable suggestions. A special debt of gratitude goes to Pakistani master calligrapher Rasheed Butt (‹http://www.RasheedButt.com/›), who generously offered to supply Arabic epigraphs for each chapter, plus the splendid *hilya* icon in Chapter 3. As always, thanks to my wife, Judith Ernst, for her tolerance, encouragement, and sound criticism.

Following
MUHAMMAD

CHAPTER 1
ISLAM IN THE EYES OF THE WEST

يُوقَدُ مِن شَجَرَةٍ مُبَارَكَةٍ

زَيْتُونَةٍ لَا شَرْقِيَّةٍ وَلَا غَرْبِيَّةٍ

Islam as Part of the Contemporary World

For more than thirty years I have been convinced that the greatest contemporary gap in understanding lies between the majority of Americans and Europeans—the so-called West—and the rest of the world. As an American exposed to international experience early (I spent a year as an exchange student to Chile at age sixteen), I came to realize that despite their many virtues, Americans are not very good at understanding other cultures. This gap in understanding is largely a one-way affair. That is, in the process we now call globalization, the products of American and European culture are broadcast to every country in the world. As a result of the era of European colonialism, languages such as French, Spanish, English, Portuguese, and Russian are the most prestigious vehicles of education and mass communication throughout Africa, the Middle East, and Asia. In contrast, it is possible for educated Americans and Europeans to ignore Chinese, Hindi-Urdu, Arabic, Bengali, and Malay-Indonesian with perfect equanimity, even though more people today speak these non-European languages.[1] While American and European authors, artists, and actors are known throughout the world, it has been a rare occurrence for an Asian, Middle Easterner, or African to obtain this kind of status.

Although globalization has been seen as the defining process of our time, we seem to be uneasy and confused about what kind of world we actually live in. It used to be that we spoke of three worlds: the First World, consisting of economically and technologically developed nations, primarily the United States, Europe, and Japan; the Second World, mainly the former Soviet

Union and its Communist allies; and the Third World, the poor and underdeveloped countries of Asia, Africa, and the Americas. It has been more than a decade since the fall of the Berlin Wall and the end of the Soviet empire, so the Second World evidently no longer exists. How many worlds are left?

Conventional wisdom has it that, despite the demise of the USSR, there is still a confrontation of the West against the rest. The chief spokesperson for this viewpoint in recent years has been Samuel Huntington, whose provocative article "The Clash of Civilizations" became a widely read book.[2] His thesis, based on a superficial and tendentious reading of history, claimed that there are a given number of civilizations (up to eight, in theory) that will inevitably clash until one emerges triumphant. After eliminating the least important of these civilizations, he concludes by postulating an eventual death struggle between the progressive West and the retrograde Islamic world.

This argument was met with dismay and concern among intellectuals and political leaders in majority Muslim countries. Only a few years ago most of these countries lay under European colonial domination, the result of aggressive European military expansion in Africa, the Middle East, and Asia since the days of Napoleon. Would this argument be used to unleash new military adventures against the enemies of "the West"? Significant voices were raised to refute this confrontational position. President Khatami of Iran responded by proposing an alternate view, which he called the "dialogue of civilizations." The United Nations adopted the formula of dialogue of civilizations as a theme for worldwide discussions in 2001.

The fact is, as American Islamic studies specialist Marshall Hodgson pointed out long ago, there has not been a separate "Muslim world" for more than 200 years. Politically, economically, culturally, and of course militarily, the fates of majority Muslim countries have been closely tied to Europe and America throughout this period. International financial networks, multinational corporations, media conglomerates, and the Internet have now created a world in which it is impossible to keep one culture isolated from the rest. If one looks at the more than fifty nations that have a majority Muslim population today, one is forced to confront a bewildering diversity of languages, ethnic groups, and differing ideological and sectarian positions (though the flow of information can still be largely in one direction). In the heart of "the West," there are today at least 5 million American Muslims and 10 million European Muslims. So why do we continue speaking of "the Muslim world" in opposition to "the West," when such a concept is out of step with reality? Do we really wish to condone the notion that there are two violently opposed worlds struggling for global domination? The extraordinary mismatch between Euro-American ideas of Islam and the realities lived by Muslims will form a recurring theme throughout this book. There is no one simple or easy explanation, though one must look both at history and at contemporary political interests to see the larger patterns.[3]

To begin with, it may be helpful to ask how we define "the West," or "Western civilization," since this phrase has no obvious geographical meaning if it includes territories as far apart as North America, Europe, and possibly Japan. As an explanation, I would put forward an academic ritual in which I was involved some twenty years ago, when as a first-year professor at Pomona College in Claremont, California, I was asked to take part in the Ceremony of the Flame. The basic structure of this ceremony was simple: a series of individuals, beginning with the chairman of the Board of Trustees, enacted a flame-passing ritual, in which the flame of knowledge and enlightenment was transmitted to the college president, a senior faculty member, a new faculty member (me), a senior student, and finally a lowly first-year student (this was originally done with lit candles but, for safety reasons, was now performed with battery-operated, candle-shaped lights). Meanwhile, an announcer read a short passage explaining the ceremony, starting with the phrase, "In the beginning, there was light." With obvious religious overtones referring to both Genesis and the Gospel of John, the narration went on to describe the gradual westward movement of this light of knowledge, until it ultimately reached its destination in the foothills of Southern California. Simultaneously, college officials symbolically passed this knowledge on to students.

Although the example may seem eccentric, it presents the essential outlines of the concept of Western civilization that is transmitted to millions of American students through history textbooks, and which is believed by many to be the essence of our culture and society. The typical sequence of this civilization's development begins briefly in Mesopotamia and Egypt before heading to Greece, where it really gets started. It is important to notice that, as civilization moves west, its preceding locations fall out and become irrelevant. After Greece declines, then comes Rome, followed by the gradual ascendancy of France, Germany, and possibly Spain. But (at least in American versions) the next destination is definitely England, followed ultimately by America as its ultimate goal. The special twist that makes California the apex of Western civilization is disputed, however, in places like New York.

Presented in this manner, the concept of Western civilization may appear ludicrous. More seriously, one might say that the defining characteristics of Western civilization are considered to derive from two sources: Israelite prophecy and revelation, on one hand, as a source of ethics and religion, and Greek philosophy and reasoning, on the other, as the basis of both science and democracy. As a straightforward historical description, this account of the origins of European civilization seems reasonably accurate. Nevertheless, if we attempt to come up with a parallel definition for Islamic civilization, we are presented with a predicament. The Islamic tradition also claims to be based on the same two sources, the prophets of Israel and the philosophers of Greece. The Qur'an acknowledges a long line of prophets including Abraham, Moses, and Jesus. Greek philosophy and science, moreover, were subjects of intense study in the lands ruled by Muslim caliphs when they were barely known in Christian Europe; it was only due to translations from Arabic into Latin that Aristotle was rediscovered in Paris and Oxford. Philosophy continued to undergo significant development, particularly in Iran and India, up to modern times (although this has been largely unknown outside specialist circles). The European and American claim to exclusive ownership of the two main sources of civilization is therefore historically false. There were also important countertrends in the symbols of civilization that moved east instead of west. After Rome itself had fallen to barbarian conquest, Constantinople (also known as Byzantium) was the capital of the ongoing Roman Empire. When the Ottoman sultans conquered Constantinople in 1453, they themselves self-consciously took on the mantle of the Roman Empire; although Western Europeans knew them as Turks, to their Arab subjects in the Near East they were simply "the Romans" ("Rumi," or "Arwam" in the plural).

This kind of cultural myopia and chauvinism is not limited to Europeans, to be sure. Writing in North Africa in the late fourteenth century, the great Arab historian and philosopher Ibn Khaldun observed that he had heard rumors that, among the northern Frankish barbarians (i.e., European Christians), there were some who were interested in philosophy, but he had never seen any proof of this. Doubtless this remark would have been highly offensive to European philosophers of the day, had they been able to read it. Today, in any case, it is no longer defensible to take refuge in ignorance as an excuse for making exclusive claims to civilization. By excluding Muslims from Western civilization, Europeans and Americans are claiming a questionable identity. Excluding Muslims from European culture in general also runs counter to history. Despite the expulsion of the Moors and Jews from medieval Spain, and the nationalistic rejection of the "Turkish yoke" in southeastern Europe in the nineteenth century, Islam has been a defining factor in European culture for more than a thousand years.[4]

Ultimately, Huntington's clash of civilizations should be seen as a reversion to colonial doctrines of European supremacy. It lacks the overt dependence on racial theory that was fashionable in the nineteenth century, but it shares the basic prejudice of reserving true civilization for Europe, which is opposed by barbarism everywhere else. The technical edge that gave Europe military superiority over the rest of the world is mistaken for cultural superiority. The 1910 edition of the *Encyclopaedia Britannica* summed up this attitude perfectly in its article on Asia written by a British colonial official:

> Asiatics stand on a higher level than the natives of Africa or America, but do not possess the special material civilization of western Europe. As far as any common mental characteristic can be assigned it is also somewhat negative, namely, that Asiatics have not the same sentiment of independence and freedom as Europeans. Individuals are thought of as members of a family, state or religion, rather than as entities with a destiny and rights of their own. This leads to autocracy in politics, fatalism in religion and conservatism in both.

While it might be conceded that most religions originated in Asia, Christian Europe had managed to cut itself clear of those origins:

Christianity, though Asiatic in its origin and essential ideas, has to a large extent taken its present form on European soil, and some of its most important manifestations—notably the Roman Church—are European reconstructions in which little of the Asiatic element remains. . . . Buddhism has never made much impression west of India, and Islam is clearly repugnant to Europeans. . . . Hence there is clearly a deep-seated difference between the religious feelings of the two continents.[5]

In its own day, this colonial rhetoric of European supremacy served as a justification for conquest and domination of the rest of the world. It is understandable that Huntington's similar thesis should cause alarm among those who are excluded from his vision of the West.

At the same time, it cannot be denied that there have been powerful voices from Muslim countries in recent years stridently proclaiming the eternal opposition of Islam and the West. What is the reason for these claims, and why should they not be given credence? My assumption throughout this book is that every claim about religion needs to be examined critically for its political implications. Religion is not a realm of facts, but a field in which every statement is contested and all claims are challenged. Religious language in the public sphere is not meant to convey information but to establish authority and legitimacy through assertion and persuasion. The Eurocentric prejudice against Islam needs to be understood as a historical justification for colonialism. In the same way, the recent use of Islamic religious language against the West should be seen as an ideological response against colonialism that deliberately uses the same language.

Religious language expressed on a mass scale is essentially rhetorical. Sweeping religious statements of extreme opposition should not be accepted on face value, especially since they generally have immediate political consequences. One always has to ask the lawyer's question about this kind of language: Who benefits from it (cui bono)? In statements that attribute political differences to fundamental religious positions, the implicit conclusion is that there is no possibility of negotiation, because religious positions are eternal and unrelated to passing events. This is convenient to both extremes in a violent struggle. On one hand, extremist movements in opposition to the state can describe their struggle as a religious quest mandated by God. Even if the extremists are few, by making such absolute claims they can justify any action, no matter how violent, because their struggle is based on truth and the fight against evil. On the other hand, governments that wish to eradicate dissent find it convenient to label their opponents as religious fanatics; this relieves governments of the responsibility to deal with legitimate grievances, because their opponents may be dismissed as irrational and incapable of responding to reason. Examples of this kind of religious rhetoric can be found in many situations ranging from Israel and Egypt to Waco. Those who attribute conflict to religion, whether they speak as opposition figures or as state authorities, do not speak for the vast majority of religious people, and indeed they contradict the history of religion. But such is the power of the mass media that these violent messages of religious opposition are carried to every corner of the world, with a powerful and persuasive effect.

Historically, there are reasons why the religious language of Islam became a vehicle for political opposition. Over centuries of colonial rule, many Far Eastern countries enthusiastically converted to European doctrines, whether Catholicism in the Philippines under Spanish rule, Protestant Christianity in Korea, Marxism in China, or the doctrine of progress and modernization in Japan. The Hindu tradition of India was in a defensive posture in the nineteenth century, under critique from British colonial administrators and Christian missionaries. Mohandas Gandhi's nonviolent nationalism, although it drew on Hindu teachings, embraced religious pluralism and a secular Indian government. Only in recent years has a Hindu fundamentalist identity emerged in India, in part as a deliberate response to Muslim fundamentalism as well as to Christian missionaries. Buddhism, though strong in certain national contexts like Sri Lanka and Tibet, was not as easily adapted to mass political movements. Apart from the Islamic tradition, one searches in vain for another indigenous symbolic resource that could furnish Asia or Africa with an easily adaptable ideology of resistance.

In some ways, the recent prominence of the word "Islam" indicates a momentous shift in religious thought, dating from the early nineteenth century. In the scale of values found in traditional theology, the Arabic term *islam* was of secondary importance. Meaning "submission (to God)," *islam* effectively denoted performing the minimum actions required in the community (generally defined as profession of faith, prayer, fasting during Ramadan, giving alms, and performing pilgrimage to Mecca). Much more important for religious identity was "faith" (*iman*), described as believing in God and everything revealed through the prophets, and all the debates of theologians revolved around how to define the faithful believer (*mu'min*). But the term "Muslim," meaning "one who has submitted (to God)," always had a corporate and social significance, indicating membership in a religious community. "Islam" therefore became practically useful as a political boundary term, both to outsiders and to insiders who wished to draw lines around themselves.

Historically, Europeans had used the term "Muhammadan" to refer to the religion of followers of the Prophet Muhammad, although Muslims regard that as an inappropriate label.[6] The term "Islam" was introduced into European languages in the early nineteenth century by Orientalists such as Edward Lane, as an explicit analogy with the modern Christian concept of religion; in this respect, "Islam" was just as much a newly invented European term as "Hinduism" and "Buddhism" were.[7] The use of the term "Islam" by non-Muslim scholars coincides with its increasing frequency in the religious discourse of those who are now called Muslims. That is, the term "Islam" became more prominent in reformist and protofundamentalist circles at approximately the same time, or shortly after, it was popularized by European Orientalists. So in a sense, the concept of Islam in opposition to the West is just as much a product of European colonialism as it is a Muslim response to that European expansionism. Despite appeals to medieval history, it is really the past two centuries that set up the conditions for today's debates regarding Islam. Comprehending the process that led to this language of opposition is an essential task for understanding this single world that we all share.

Anti-Islamic Attitudes from Medieval Times to the Present

It is safe to say that no religion has such a negative image in Western eyes as Islam. Although it would be pointless to engage in competition between religious stereotypes, one can certainly see Gandhi and his advocacy of nonviolence as a positive image of Hinduism. Likewise, the Dalai Lama has an amazingly positive and widespread recognition as a representative of Buddhism. Europe and America have done a dramatic about-face with respect to Judaism over the course of the past century. Although anti-Semitism was common and even fashionable early in the twentieth century, the horrors of the Holocaust and the establishment of the state of Israel changed that. While anti-Semitism still lingers among certain hate groups, there are plenty of defenders of Judaism on the alert against them. Christianity, of course, remains the majority religious category in most of Europe and America, and it is not in any real danger. Among major religious groups, there remains Islam, with a complex of media images that is almost uniformly negative. How did this negative representation come to be, and what is its relationship with the actuality of Muslims past and present?[8]

This question of anti-Muslim stereotypes looms especially large today in terms of sheer numbers. No respectable authorities defend anti-Semitism anymore, and there is a widespread consensus that insulting statements and stereotypes about Jews are both factually incorrect and morally reprehensible, whether in reference to physical appearance or behavior. Yet at the same time, it is commonly accepted among educated people that Islam is a religion that by definition oppresses women and encourages violence. It is interesting to contrast these two examples from a numerical standpoint. The world population of Jews is commonly estimated at about 17 million people, somewhat less than the world population of Sikhs. Clearly, it would be ridiculous to assume that such a large number of people would all have the characteristics assumed by stereotypes. Yet the world Muslim population is well over 1 billion. It would seem to be a far greater fallacy to paint this much larger group with the same brush. Muslims are the majority population in more than fifty countries that vary widely in language, ethnic composition, natural resources, and level of technology, and they form significant minorities in many other countries. Why, then, should it be so natural for non-Muslims to assume that all Muslims are and act the same, regardless of the conditions in which they live? Is it conceivable that all Muslims are identical, and that they have no location in time and space?

The history of Christian attitudes toward Islam has been largely negative, although not always so. At the beginning of the emergence of Muslim community, Muhammad advised a small group of his followers to flee Mecca to avoid persecution at the hands of the pagan rulers of the city. The Christian king of Abyssinia received them and gave them refuge, being persuaded of their religious sincerity. In biographies of Muhammad, one frequently finds reference to his encounter with a Christian monk named Bahira during Muhammad's travels as a merchant. The monk is said to have recognized in Muhammad the signs of a prophet as predicted in Christian scriptures. Later on, however, this story was given a precisely opposite twist in the hands of hostile Christian writers, and the monk was portrayed as a renegade heretic who aided Muhammad in fraudulently claiming prophecy.

The brief remarks that follow focus mainly on Christian attitudes toward Islam, since they have had a much greater effect on the modern climate of opinion than the perspectives of Jews. Jews and Muslims typically had much more positive relations with each other in premodern times than either group had with Christians; it is really only since the establishment of the state of Israel that Jews and Muslims have become antagonistic. From a religious point of view, it is remarkable that only in recent times have Christian theologians attempted a more positive evaluation of Islam. The great series of Catholic councils of the 1960s called Vatican II produced major revisions of church doctrine, including recognition for the first time of the possibility of salvation outside the church. Yet it was only very tentatively that the published documents accorded any positive remarks to Islam, praising Muslims who practice a spiritual way of life and noting that Muslims revere the Virgin Mary. Not a word was said about the Prophet Muhammad, however.[9] Ecumenical German theologian Hans Küng was probably the first

Catholic to make a serious attempt to come to terms with Muhammad.[10]

Throughout the medieval period, all of the characteristics of the Prophet Muhammad that confirmed his authenticity in the eyes of Muslims were reversed by Christian authors and turned into defects. They simply could not tolerate the notion of a new prophet after Christ. The traditional doctrine that Muhammad was illiterate, which to Muslims was proof of the divine origin of the scripture he transmitted, indicated to Christians that he must have been a fraud. Muhammad's descent from Abraham's son Ishmael was a part of traditional Arab genealogy, and Muslims viewed this as an additional confirmation of his status; Christians considered this claim to be completely false. When challenged by the pagan Meccans to produce miracles, Muhammad had answered that the Qur'an was his only miracle. While Muslims viewed this as proof of the spirituality of his mission, Christian antagonists considered this lack of miracles as clear evidence that he was not a prophet.

The two biggest Christian criticisms of the Prophet Muhammad were undoubtedly in relation to his military activities and his marriages. For Christians, the celibacy and nonviolent approach of Jesus are generally seen as indispensable characteristics of true spirituality. The fact that Muhammad engaged in battle and was married to a number of women seems to many Christians clear proof that he could not be on the same exalted level as Jesus. Christian critics of Muhammad generally describe him as motivated by a combination of political ambition and sensual lust, hardly what one expects in a prophet. Muslims approach this issue from an entirely different direction. For them, Muhammad provides the ideal model of a prophet, who leads his people by example and demonstrates in his person how life should be lived in the world. Since life on this earth will always be subject to conflict, it is essential to have an example of the best ethical conduct of war and politics. Likewise, since human life requires procreation and the family, there must be a religious model in this area as well. Therefore, to Muslims, the Christian emphasis on Jesus' celibacy and nonviolence seems to be a completely unrealistic model that no one can follow and that ultimately ends up being hypocritical by recommending practices that are never followed. Indeed, according to some Muslim traditions, Jesus (who did not die on the Cross but is still alive in heaven) will return at the resurrection and complete his prophetic mission, during which time he will marry and judge according to the law.

The discrepancy between these two religious perspectives on Muhammad could hardly be starker. From a historical perspective, it is understandable that Christian theologians would find it unacceptable to admit the possibility of a prophet who was not sanctioned by the church or by clear expectation from scripture. Likewise, Muslim scholars regarded the Christian churches as having gone seriously astray in their interpretation of Jesus, particularly in the doctrine of the Trinity and the assertion that Jesus was the son of God. For them, the unity of God was absolutely essential, and calling a human being divine was a kind of idolatry amounting to polytheism. Nevertheless, the contrast between the Muslim and Christian perspectives here has a strange lack of symmetry. Muslims revere Jesus as a prophet of God, a human being, to be sure, but one who had a lofty spiritual status as the Messiah and the Word of God and who was born to Mary of a virgin birth. When Christians refer to Muhammad as a fraud and worse, it is extremely hurtful to Muslims because of the deep affection and reverence in which they hold him. For Muslims, Muhammad is the most compassionate one, the Prophet who alone will intercede with God for the forgiveness, not just of Muslims, but of all humanity on the Day of Judgment. Muslims are often bewildered by the extreme hostility that Christians have shown toward their beloved Prophet, and they ask what they have done to deserve such distrust, when they pay the highest compliments to Jesus. What is there in Christianity that rejects the spirituality of a man who is a lover and a fighter?

Although there have been some Christian writers who provided accurate and even unbiased accounts of the life of Muhammad, the tendency has been to go to a negative extreme that even includes fantasy and outright lies. For example, knowing that Islamic law considers both pork and alcohol to be unlawful, Christian writers circulated outrageously false reports about the death of Muhammad, asserting either that he died while drunk or that he was killed by pigs. It is hard to avoid characterizing these stories as anything but malicious. Likewise, in romantic epics such as the French *Song of Roland*, Muhammad is portrayed as a heathen idol who is worshiped like the Greek gods. In other accounts he is said to have been a renegade cardinal of the Catholic Church who decided to start his own false religion. This image of Muhammad as an unprincipled Christian renegade underlies his depiction in Dante's *Inferno* (canto 28:31–36), where Muhammad and his son-in-law ʿAli appear in Hell with the "disseminators of scandal and of schism," with demons splitting their heads open in punishment. Curiously enough, Dante had reserved a place for the Muslim philosophers Avicenna and Averroes in Limbo, along with the virtuous pagan Greeks and Romans (4:143–44), but he was not troubled by this particular inconsistency. The Protestant reformer Martin Luther called Muhammad, among other things, the devil's son, and it was typical for other Christian writers to refer to him as the Antichrist.[11]

The main political context for anti-Muslim writings by European Christians in the Middle Ages was undoubtedly the Crusades. The attempts of Christian princes, with the blessing of the

Roman Catholic Church, to conquer the holy lands that were occupied by Arabs and Turks are among the strangest episodes in European history. A military and religious movement that lasted for several centuries, the Crusades had many unexpected outcomes, such as regular massacres of Jews and the sacking of the Orthodox Christian city of Constantinople. Although they had a tremendous effect on western Europe, the ultimately un-successful Crusader attacks had much less significance in the Near East, where they were often viewed as one more series of raids by northern barbarians. It was particularly in the Mediter-ranean West and in Spain that the crusading mentality reached its highest intensity. The Spanish Reconquista was a gradual frontier conquest carried out over centuries with the full sup-port of the pope, culminating in the conquest of Granada in 1492 and the eventual expulsion or forced conversion of the Moors (Andalusian Muslims) along with the Jews. The anti-Muslim policy of the Spanish kings was, coincidentally, the basis for the support of the voyage of Columbus to America in the same year, as a way of outflanking the Muslim control of the East Indies spice trade. Meanwhile, in southeastern Europe, the Ottoman Turks captured Constantinople in 1453 and began an aggressive campaign of conquest of the Balkan countries, threatening central Europe as late as the seventeenth century. English writers of the early 1600s viewed the Ottomans with fear and alarm, seeing them as a superpower threatening to over-whelm all of Europe.[12]

Although the medieval Christian background of the Cru-sades continued to have influence, it is not sufficient, by itself, to explain modern anti-Muslim prejudices. For that, we have to turn to the modern colonial period. For Americans in particular it is important to draw attention to colonialism as a distinctive feature of modernity. America's own colonial period is far in the past and is not remembered as being particularly stressful. For most Americans, the word "colonial" conjures up quaint images of reconstructed theme parks like Williamsburg. They are not familiar with the far more efficient systems of colonial rule that the French and British developed in the nineteenth century, with powerful support in technology, policing, and racial ideology. To gauge the impact of colonialism, it may suffice to cite a single example: Algeria, which France invaded and conquered in 1830. It is estimated that during the ultimately successful Algerian war of independence (1954–62), well more than 1 million Algerians were killed, while probably 30,000 Frenchmen died during the same period. Colonialism, in short, was based on brutal and efficient military conquest.

Still, America's own initial encounters with Islam took place in largely colonial contexts. One of these was the African slave trade, since as many as 15 percent of the West Africans sold into slavery in the United States were Muslims, including a number who preserved their culture and even wrote texts in Arabic while enslaved in the South (see fig. 1.1). Another important case was America's colonial occupation of the Philippines, which lasted from the Spanish-American War in 1898 through World War II. Most of the military activity that American troops saw in the Philippines during the Spanish-American War was directed against resistance by Muslim tribesmen. It was this American intervention in the Philippines that led Rudyard Kipling to write his famous ode to colonialism, "The White Man's Burden." Although most Americans today have forgotten this episode, leading contemporary figures such as Mark Twain and Andrew Carnegie vehemently opposed this military adventure and its colonial aftermath.[13] In situations like these, America has been very much involved with modern colonialism and confrontation with Muslims, particularly in places such as Iran and Egypt, where the United States has stepped into the shoes formerly occupied by the British.

FIGURE 1.1

*Photograph of Omar ibn Sayyid (1772–1864), a West African
Muslim scholar sold into slavery in 1807, who wrote his Arabic
autobiography on a North Carolina plantation (North Carolina
Collection, University of North Carolina Library at Chapel Hill)*

As the power of the Ottoman Empire waned and it was no longer seen as a serious threat, European colonial expansion into Asia and Africa became more extensive. When Napoleon invaded Egypt in 1798, he briefly toyed with the idea of converting to Islam and conquering Asia, becoming another Alexander; true to the French way of life, however, he rejected this fancy when he learned he would have to give up wine. In the era of the Enlightenment, with its rejection of religious authority, new justifications for conquest were needed beyond the notion of religious crusade. Science and rationality furnished the new basis for empire. Military technology, in which Europe had definitely seized the advantage, permitted forcible conquest of the rest of the world. The scientific doctrine of race, in particular, provided a rationalization for Europe's domination of the world. Thinkers such as Auguste Comte proclaimed that five advanced European nations (England, France, Italy, Spain, and Germany) constituted the vanguard of humanity. Charles Darwin's theory of evolution was applied in ways indicating that white Europeans were more highly evolved than the rest of humanity and hence were obliged to rule. For the British it was the "white man's burden," while for the French it was the "civilizing mission." Karl Marx and Friedrich Engels formulated the theory of the "Oriental mode of production," and it was commonly accepted that peoples of the East were by nature suited to "Oriental despotism."

The remarkable strength of racial theory during this time can be seen in an extraordinary exchange that took place between one of the leading European scholars of Islamic studies and a Muslim reformer. Ernst Renan, a leading scholar in Paris and author of important works on medieval philosophy, delivered a lecture at the Sorbonne in 1883 in which he argued that Islam was incompatible with science and philosophy. He based his reasoning on the claim that Islam was an essentially Arab religion and that Arabs belong to the Semitic race, which has an "atomistic" mentality that is incapable of philosophical synthesis. As it happened, the Muslim reformer Jamal al-Din Afghani was in Paris at the time seeking temporary respite from a tumultuous political career. Afghani challenged Renan's conclusion, although he accepted the notion that all religions are basically authoritarian and antiscientific; Islam was a younger tradition than Christianity, he argued, and so it would just take a little longer for the scientific spirit to emerge. In his response to Afghani, Renan generously observed that his critic was doubtless capable of philosophical thinking because as an Afghan he was of Aryan racial stock. Nevertheless, Renan remained firmly convinced that Semites (meaning Arabs and Jews) did not have this capacity. Anti-Semitism and racial doctrines of this type were not only common in the nineteenth century but even fashionable.[14]

This is not to say that Christian missionary activity ceased during the colonial period; to the contrary, the nineteenth century was probably the high point of systematic organization of Christian missions to the world. Christian missionaries honed their ability in countless local languages, partly to translate the Bible into these tongues and partly to debate the truth of Christianity and the falsity of other religions. The style, the vocabulary, and the arguments of the missionaries would have a tremendous influence in molding the ways in which many non-Christians (including Muslims) defended their faiths.

While Christian religious concepts doubtless still influenced the thinking of colonial administrators, the main emphasis was on European culture and science as the apex of human progress. A revealing document in this context is the famous "Minute on Indian Education" delivered by Thomas Babington Macaulay in 1835 as a justification for making English the standard language of education throughout British India. This is what he had to say about the classical languages of Arabic and Sanskrit used by Muslims and Hindus:

> I have no knowledge of either Sanscrit or Arabic. — But I have done what I could to form a correct estimate of their value. I have read translations of the most celebrated Arabic and Sanscrit works. I have conversed both here and at home with men distinguished by their proficiency in the Eastern tongues. I am quite ready to take the Oriental learning at the valuation of the Orientalists themselves. I have never found one among them who could deny that a single shelf of a good European library was worth the whole native literature of India and Arabia. The intrinsic superiority of the Western literature is, indeed, fully admitted by those members of the Committee who support the Oriental plan of education.[15]

Another telling example was William Muir's *Life of Mahomet* (1858), written by a British colonial official in India at the suggestion of a Christian missionary who specialized in debating with Muslims. In this biography Muir not only entertained the suggestion that Muhammad was inspired by the devil, but he also adopted the more scientific criticism (originally advanced by German physician Aloys Sprenger) that Muhammad's prophetic experiences were due to epilepsy.[16] As far as these colonial administrators were concerned, the study of the religion of their subjects was important insofar as it might pose a challenge to European authority.[17]

During the same period that saw the rise of European colonialism, the academic study of Africa and Asia became established in European universities. The study of anything in the East was called Orientalism, and this term to some extent lumped together everything non-European. Much of this scholarly enterprise was based on detailed study of difficult languages and texts, so that it was not easily accessible outside specialized academic publications and caused little controversy. In recent years, however, there has been considerable debate about Orientalism, largely fueled by the provocative 1978 book of that title by Edward Said.[18] Were Orientalist scholars complicit agents assisting the imperialist enterprise of European conquest? Was their portrait of the East, particularly Muslim countries, essentially designed to facilitate the domination of those countries? This would be an exaggeration. Most of those scholars, of many nationalities, were unworldly persons who thought of their academic work as similar to the study of Greek and Latin. Until very recently it never occurred to most Orientalist scholars that their work might have implications for the lives of contemporary Muslims.

Nevertheless, certain Orientalist ideas common in the nineteenth century have contributed to current stereotypes about Islam.[19] One of these preconceptions is the idea that Oriental cultures are animated fundamentally by religious and spiritual impulses. This concept of the "mystic East," which came from European Romanticism, contributed to a tendency to disregard more mundane factors such as technology, economics, and society. Similarly, Orientalist scholars tended to accept nineteenth-century racial theories unquestioningly, so that much of Near Eastern and Asian history was explained in terms of primordial conflicts between the Semitic and Indo-Aryan races (for example, Arabs against Persians). In addition, it was widely believed that the properties of language had a deep and essential impact on religion and culture, so that from a study of the Arabic language one would be able to predict and perfectly comprehend the nature of the Islamic religion or Arab culture today. All these tendencies contributed to the assumption that armchair scholars in their European libraries could come to a definitive understanding of the essentially unchanging realities of Islamic religion, Semitic and Aryan races, and Oriental languages. All that one really needed was a dictionary and some Arabic manuscripts, and there was no need to consider issues such as contemporary history, economic class, social status, or the opinions of natives. At the same time, colonial officials in Muslim regions tended to believe that any resistance to their authority must derive from Muslim religious fanaticism rather than any natural opposition to foreign political control. It is easy to see in retrospect how Orientalist assumptions about Islam could play into the justification of European colonialism. Much of this nineteenth-century scholarship is still available in print, since it is not copyrighted. Thus it continues to be recycled and has an impact today far greater than it deserves.

In more recent history, undoubtedly the most important factor in creating stereotypes about Arabs and Muslims has been the Zionist movement and the Arab-Israeli conflict. It is ironic that Zionism, which began as a socialist movement led by secular Jews, has become a defining element in Jewish religious identity. From a historical perspective, Zionism is a classic European nationalist movement with a colonial implementation. The first theorist of Jewish nationalism, Moses Hess (d. 1875), was a socialist and a close associate of Karl Marx. The early Zionist movement, under the leadership of Theodore Herzl (d. 1905), formulated a national identity for Jews focused on the return to the traditional homeland around Jerusalem. Large-scale Jewish immigration from Europe and Russia to Palestine gathered momentum following World War I, after Britain took control of portions of the former Ottoman Empire. In its scale and pioneer attitude, the establishment of Jewish settlements in British Palestine, with European support, was comparable to the French colonization of Algeria.

The horrors of the Holocaust gave urgency to the Zionist movement after World War II, and British withdrawal from its colonies led to the 1947 independence of Israel, the first of several wars with adjoining Arab countries, and the creation of an enormous Palestinian refugee population. American attitudes toward the state of Israel have been heavily colored by Protestant evangelical Christianity, assisted by pro-Israel American Jewish groups. Many Americans do not make much distinction between the ancient Israelites of the Bible and the modern nation-state. Israel figures dramatically in recent apocalyptic speculations based on the Book of Daniel and the Book of Revelation, such as Hal Lindsay's best-selling book, *The Late Great Planet Earth*. These contemporary interpretations of biblical prophecy frequently include predictions of the destruction of Muslim monuments in Jerusalem in order to permit the rebuilding of the Solomonic temple, the advent of the Messiah, and the events of the Last Days. Israeli authorities, who likewise draw upon the symbolism of ancient Israel, have found it convenient to encourage this Christian belief, despite the demise of Judaism envisioned in these apocalyptic scenarios. American Christians therefore generally instinctively support the state of Israel against Palestinians, despite the significant minority of Palestinians who are Christians.[20]

Since Israel's 1967 conquest of the West Bank and the Gaza Strip, it has controlled these Palestinian territories through colonial mechanisms inherited from the British. The Occupied Territories are practically the only place left where repressive British colonial laws are still being applied, permitting land seizure, mass punishments, destruction of suspects' homes, denial of building permits, and the like. Palestinian resistance to Israeli occupation took the form of leftist secular national liberation movements like the Palestine Liberation Organization. It is a serious mistake to call this conflict religious or to regard it as rooted in primordial religious attitudes. The conflict between Jews and Arabs is a contemporary dispute about ownership of the land, and it is a product of the past century. It is only in recent years that religious fundamentalism has taken hold as a force among a portion of the Palestinians, with the rise of the Hamas movement and groups such as Islamic Jihad. Spectacular acts of violence committed by Palestinian commandos in the 1960s and 1970s firmly established the image of the Arab as terrorist. These Palestinians were secular, and Arabs are a minority of Muslims; yet to the average American newspaper reader, "Arab," "Muslim," and "terrorist" have become almost interchangeable terms. In the absence of any contact with real Arabs or Muslims in daily life, many have accepted this kind of violent image as a substitute, as if there could be an entire society composed of terrorists.

Without attempting to trace the further history of these stereotypes, I must say something here about one of the most powerful images of all: the veiled woman, an image often tinged with erotic fantasies. As we have seen, accusations of lascivious behavior was one of the stock charges that Christians made against the Prophet Muhammad. The possibility of a man marrying as many as four wives under Islamic law, though uncommon in practice, also fed the imagination of Christian clerics. New material for fantasizing about Arab and Muslim women became available with Jean Antoine Galland's French translation of the *Thousand and One Nights* (published 1704–17), which created a craze for Oriental tales. In the nineteenth century, French Orientalist painters created luxuriant depictions of seductive harem life, using European prostitutes as nude models. The conservative clothing worn by many Near Eastern women (including Eastern Christians and Jews through the nineteenth century) and the segregation of unrelated men and women in public spaces also encouraged male European travelers with overactive imaginations.

Although modern Europeans and Americans assume that Muslim women are invariably oppressed, it is by no means clear that Muslim women have always suffered from disadvantages in comparison with Christians or others. This is an instance in which very recent advances in Europe and America are somehow assumed to be an essential part of the West. English women did not have full property rights until the Married Women's Property Acts of 1870 and 1882, yet under Islamic law, Muslim women have been guaranteed inheritance and property rights since the seventh century. English women were still chattels of their husband or father when Lady Mary Wortley Montagu traveled to Constantinople in 1716 with her husband, the British ambassador. She was amazed to meet there Ottoman women of the nobility who owned large estates and managed their own property without male interference. Lady Mary even found the veil to be a liberating device that freed women from the prying eyes of men. Certainly misogyny and unequal rights for women are features that can be found in abundance in the societies of North Africa, the Near East, and much of Asia, but can we honestly say that America and Europe are free of these problems? It is easy and hypocritical to accuse other societies of abuses and inequities when injustices still exist in our own culture. The image of the oppressed Muslim woman can all too often serve as another self-righteous reason for Europeans to congratulate themselves on their superiority.

In all the images of Islam that are commonly circulated in European and American culture, little can be found that is positive. Is it possible for an entire civilization to have such negative features, enduring more than 1,000 years across half the world? Although I am not a psychologist, I cannot help but feel that there is a mechanism of projection operating here, along the lines spoken of by Jungians, in which one's own negative characteristics are projected onto others. There is certainly plenty of evidence of fantasy throughout the history of anti-Islamic stereotypes. Muslims are considered to be violent, yet we do not hear any similar accusations about intrinsic violence in Christianity or European culture; what was it about Christianity that motivated the world conquests of the nineteenth century or more recent atrocities such as the 1996 massacre of more than 6,000 Muslim men and boys carried out in a single day by Eastern Orthodox Serbs in Srebrenica? Muslims are considered to have dysfunctional roles for women, yet that emblem of Western technological superiority, the Internet, is saturated with pornographic images, and the sexualization of women is omnipresent in television, newspapers, and advertising. Is the West so confident of its relations between the sexes? Everyone needs to become educated as a media critic nowadays, because the recycling of sensational images is what the communications media love most, especially when conflict is present. Islam is a subject that most Americans and Europeans have experienced only through these negative images and stereotypes. Clearly the time has come to go beyond those images and encounter real human beings.

Avoiding Prejudice in Approaching Islam

It is a premise of this book that all Muslims are not the same. Like any other large cross section of humanity, they are affected by the major factors of life that influence us all: economic class, access to political power, ethnicity, gender, nationality, location, language, and history. To assume that Muslims, and Muslims alone, are driven to act exclusively by religion, apart from any of the other factors that shape our lives, is more than absurd. It dehumanizes Muslims and makes them into frightening monsters who are not only alien but also hostile. It means that there are no legitimate grievances that need to be considered by non-

Muslims. It means that Muslims have no history, and therefore others have no obligation to understand them. If all Muslims are violent fanatics, there is only one possible response to them: violent confrontation.

Both the assumptions and the conclusions of these anti-Muslim stereotypes are repugnant to reason and justice. Yet these negative stereotypes of Islam have a history that has been deeply embedded in the self-images of Euro-American societies. Islamophobia has succeeded anti-Semitism as a form of acceptable racial and religious prejudice.[21] There are important political reasons for the existence of these stereotypes, and particular interests are served by their perpetuation. Yet if we are to construct a vision of the world in which multiple cultures exist together without confrontation or domination, it is necessary that non-Muslims should be able to understand the perspectives of Muslims.

Here one may be tempted to ask, Is it not also necessary that Muslims should understand the perspectives of non-Muslims? Fairness and reciprocity certainly demand that understanding be mutual. An important historical clarification focusing on the high point of European colonialism is necessary at this point. During this period, from Napoleon's invasion of Egypt (1798) to the end of World War I and the dismemberment of the Ottoman Empire, the main European powers (plus Russia and China) engaged in a systematic military conquest of Muslim countries. This process subjected nearly 90 percent of the world Muslim population to colonial control. The only countries that were not conquered outright were Arabia, Persia, Turkey, and Afghanistan. Two major conclusions may be drawn from the series of events. First, Muslims subjected to colonialism became intimately familiar with their non-Muslim rulers and the European culture they imposed. These Europeans overthrew native dynasties, dismantled traditional systems of education, enforced centralized authoritarian rule, and trained new local elites in the new languages of power—English, French, Dutch, Italian, Portuguese, and Russian. Second, the process of violent conquest was undertaken by largely Christian powers, yet paradoxically it is the Muslims who are regarded as naturally violent. Again, this appears to be a kind of projection, but on a massive scale, suggesting that there is something seriously flawed in the self-understanding of Euro-Americans in relation to Muslims.

In order to approach an alternative to the negative stereotypes of Islam and Muslims, it is necessary for the reader to take a journey not only through the main topics of the Islamic religion but also beyond religion. Religion never exists in a vacuum. It is always interwoven with multiple strands of culture and history that link it to particular locations. The rhetoric of religion must be put into a context, so that we know both the objectives and the opponents of particular spokespeople.

To take one example that will be expanded upon later, Islamic law has become a highly charged and controversial topic in a number of countries with majority Muslim populations. Certain ideologues (those whose theological positions require them to take power) have announced their aim as the establishment of pure Islamic law. They present themselves as returning to the standards established by the Prophet Muhammad 1,400 years ago, ruling society exclusively on the basis of the Qur'an. This audacious claim, which was never made before the twentieth century, reflects the very modern rhetoric of fundamentalism. It flies in the face of Islamic history, since every premodern political regime that we know of combined Islamic law with local custom, pre-Islamic structures, and administrative decrees. In addition, European powers dismantled the apparatus of Islamic law in the countries that they conquered, leaving only certain drastically modified sections applying to personal and family law. Therefore, at present, formerly colonized countries (such as Egypt, India, or Algeria) have mixed legal codes primarily based on European law. Countries that claim to have purely Islamic systems, on closer scrutiny, look rather different. Saudi Arabia has a monarchy plus a considerable admixture of pre-Islamic Arabian tribal custom, and Iran has a modern constitutional government structure combined with clerical rule. In a much more extreme case, the Taliban government in Afghanistan, in forbidding women to be educated or to appear in public, distorted both custom and Islamic law to a level that is unprecedented and even pathological.

To present, therefore, a contextual understanding of Islam, it is necessary to continually take up particular examples and ask how symbols and concepts from the Islamic tradition are reinterpreted and reapplied in new situations. An important case is the concept of jihad, often mistranslated as "holy war." It would be more appropriate to explain this word as meaning "struggle for truth." Over the centuries this ethical ideal has been held up as the quest for virtue in a variety of forms. It has a secondary meaning of military struggle against evil opponents, and it was inevitably appropriated in a self-serving fashion by many royal dynasties seeking justification for their conquests. Thus, for example, the Persian shah and the Ottoman sultan did not hesitate to declare that each was waging a righteous "struggle for truth" against the other, when in practice one kingdom was simply battling another as usual. The subject of jihad will be explored in greater depth below, but the point is that religious symbols have no specific meaning in themselves apart from the people who deliberately employ them in specific ways.

To put the matter of historical context more bluntly, in every issue that has to do with Islam, the most important question revolves around who is authorized to interpret Islam. There is, after all, no Muslim pope. Should everyone accept the authority of the religious leaders in Saudi Arabia? Some Muslims reject those scholars because they consider the puritanical Wahhabi doctrine to be extremist, and even the Saudi government has announced that edicts regarding Islamic law are only acceptable from officially recognized scholars. What about important figures such as Ayatollah Khomeini, the inspiration of the Iranian revolution? Although his opinions were considered binding by the minority of Muslims who are Shi'i, and despite the international admiration he attracted for his anti-imperialist stand, his religious authority had no currency for the majority of Muslims who consider themselves Sunni. Or should one listen to the authorities in Egypt's most ancient and prestigious theological academy, al-Azhar University? Here, too, there are many who reject the authority of these scholars on the grounds that they are overly dependent on the Egyptian government and all too likely to reproduce the official state perspective. In short, regardless of claims of absolute authority, there is no one perspective that is recognized throughout Muslim countries. Therefore, anyone who wants to avoid being gullible needs to exercise some critical judgment regarding any comprehensive statement about Islam, particularly when it is presented as "*the* Islamic view on . . . ."

In approaching Islamic texts and religious concepts, one must stand aside from the attitude of missionary competition that underlies the modern concept of religion. That is, it is all too easy to fall into the trap of using isolated quotations of scripture or law as "proof texts" to determine the acceptability or unacceptability of an entire religion. There are cheap debater's tricks of this type that are easily abused by those who have an ax to grind, but it is much easier to detect unfair citations when you are already familiar with the tradition. Thus one could take a passage from the New Testament, like St. Paul's insistence (in I Corinthians) that women should cover their hair and keep silent in church; reading this, readers with feminist inclinations might conclude that any religion containing such a rule is unacceptable. Such a single-issue approach based on current orthodoxies tends to limit, at the very least, one's ability to understand the meaning and significance of this verse in its own time and place. Contemporary Christians might reply that it was a custom for respectable married women to wear head coverings at that time. They might also argue that there are other verses about the equality of the sexes that are statements of principle and therefore more important than this acknowledgment of contemporary fashion. Regardless of the details of this example, it is important to engage in a certain amount of patient questioning when confronted with things that seem strange to contemporary sensibilities.

In the same way, those who are intent on finding proof texts to demonstrate the necessarily evil intentions of Muslims should be aware that they themselves are using the methods and arguments of fundamentalism. For instance, one can find texts from the Qur'an proclaiming war against the pagan Arabs of Mecca, who were engaged in a bitter struggle against Muhammad, and these have been used as evidence that Muslims are perennially engaged in warfare against all non-Muslims. Yet few would hold that the more bloodthirsty passages of the Hebrew Bible require all Jews and Christians to emulate verses like the following: "If I whet my glittering sword, and my hand takes hold on judgment, I will take vengeance on my adversaries, and will requite those who hate me. I will make my arrows drunk with blood, and my sword shall devour flesh—with the blood of the slain and the captives, from the long-haired heads of the enemy" (Deut. 32:41–42). One can also find places in the New Testament where Jesus uses alarming language: "Do not think that I have come to bring peace on earth; I have not come to bring peace, but a sword" (Matt. 10:34). While there may be fundamentalists who insist on the unlimited applicability of every verse of this type, most Jews and Christians would assert that such sayings reflect particular historical situations and are limited to those contexts. They would further argue that there are overriding moral themes and principles in the Bible that take precedence over individual verses, or that metaphorical or allegorical language is being used in certain cases. It would seem only reasonable that, instead of leaping to the most alarming conclusions, we allow Muslims the opportunity to interpret their own scripture. Yet few outsiders have bothered to discover the history of Qur'anic interpretation among Muslims, especially since only fundamentalist versions of Islam have come to the attention of the mass media.

It is also important to recall that a number of significant features of modern society have come into existence relatively recently. Slavery, for instance, is accepted in the Bible as a normal part of life; American slave owners used the Bible both to justify slavery and to convince slaves to accept their lot as God's will. Democracy, human rights, and women's rights are not mentioned in any ancient scriptures. Religious tolerance is a secular attitude stemming from the Enlightenment's resentment against the abuse of religious authority. Thus many typical features of modern life are recent historical developments that owe little to traditional religion. Yet these undeniable advances for humanity have recently been accepted, for the most part, in major religious traditions. It is very easy to assume that our contemporary society is the norm, and then if we encounter something markedly different, there is a tendency to reject it with a smug sense of superiority. An example would be the well-known punishment of theft in Islamic law by cutting off the hand. It would be a standard modern reaction to be repulsed and call it barbaric, as bad as the harsh criminal punishments that were prevalent in most of Europe 300 years ago, though we tend to be anthropologically blind to examples so close at hand.

Yet this simple recitation of what is supposed to be Islamic law leaves out several extremely important factors from the history of its practice: the tendency to restrict the application of punishments of this category, the high standard of evidence demanded (including unimpeachable eyewitnesses), the acceptability of plausible excuses, and a strong reluctance to apply this punishment if there were mitigating circumstances such as poverty or sincere repentance. Modern readers would assume this is an inflexible legal code, but in fact Muslim judges had considerable independence in how they interpreted and applied the law; the history of the application of this law in different regions and times would reveal much about changes in the role of Islamic law in those societies. The situation is entirely changed, however, when zealous self-taught ideologues make amputation of the hand the standard punishment for every case of theft or prosecute rape victims on charges of adultery (classical law required the testimony of four adult male eyewitnesses to the act of adultery, an unlikely possibility). The extreme application of these punishments is, for some, an outstanding credential of the authentic Islamic state, even though it stands traditional doctrine and practice on its head. As one scholar observes, "When Islamic law is reduced to excessive manifestations, it becomes, for its adamant advocates, a provocative tool against the rest of the world, and the West in particular (this is primarily what sets us apart, and it must be emphasized), and a weapon of intolerance in their own societies (whoever opposes us over the sacred law is an apostate). Islamic law becomes, in this approach, the focus of the impending clash of civilizations."[22] This ideological imposition of *shari'a*, with none of the safeguards of the Islamic legal tradition, is rightly seen as a travesty.

All this is to indicate that no religious concept, symbol, or practice is self-evident; in every case, one needs to ask about the situation in which a particular aspect of Islam is being invoked. Likewise, in the proliferation of online texts that characterizes the contemporary information age, it is especially important to read critically the controversial material that appears on Internet sites attacking and condemning opposed points of view.[23] Since anyone with a few hours to spare can create a website that looks reasonably impressive, it is possible for any extremist or eccentric to present one-sided and distorting material in a way that makes it look acceptable. In the culture of the Internet, religious advocacy websites, as a category, are closer to advertising websites than any other kind. One needs to ask questions about the purposes of such websites and about the identities of their authors in order to distinguish missionaries and partisans from neutral sources of information. In light of the long history of negative portrayals and distortions of Islam by hostile outside critics, it is particularly necessary to question contemporary material that plays into this extraordinarily strong anti-Islamic bias. Just as in the case of racial prejudice against blacks or anti-Semitism against Jews, the gross negative stereotyping of centuries of religious thought and hundreds of millions of people should be treated as a contemptible form of bigotry.

CHAPTER 2
APPROACHING ISLAM IN TERMS OF RELIGION

أدين بدين الحبّ أنّى توجّهت   ركائبه فالحبّ ديني وإيماني

Islam and the Modern Concept of Religion

One of the goals of this book is to raise the level of the understanding of Islam from the perspective of religion, yet this is no easy task. How can one define the concept of religion? Like any other word, "religion" has a history. The term came into existence at a certain time for certain purposes, and its meaning has changed significantly over the years. Although it may be tempting to regard major concepts such as religion as being universal and applicable in all times and places, they are, in fact, historically conditioned and depend on particular circumstances. We cannot understand religion in a timeless sense or through an abstract definition. Religion can be understood only with respect to context: we have to understand the actors, the time, the place, and the issues in order to avoid making serious mistakes.

Surprisingly, religion is not mentioned in the Bible. The word is derived from a pre-Christian Latin term, *religio*, which was adopted by European Christians in the western Mediterranean region. It is surprisingly difficult to find an equivalent term in any of the other classical languages of Christianity, such as Greek, and it is even more difficult to find comparable concepts outside Christian sources. A brief excursion into the history of this term and some of its principal transformations illustrates how dramatically a fundamental term can change. While this sketch considerably simplifies the development of the concept of religion in the West, it demonstrates how our concept of multiple religions is closely linked to the modern period of European colonialism.

One of the most important authors in ancient Rome, Cicero,

offered an explanation of the origin of the term "religion" in his Latin treatise *On the Nature of the Gods*, written around 45 B.C.E.[1] According to this explanation, the Latin term *religio* was derived from the word *relegere*, which means "to read again," or "to read over and over." Thus *religio* means a painstaking sense of duty, concentrating fully on what one is supposed to do. We still retain a sense of this usage in our expression, "He reads the daily paper religiously." It was most common for Latin writers to use the word in the plural, in the form *religiones*, meaning ritual duties. There was not necessarily any theological or doctrinal content to this concept of religion, but it did contain a notion of duty and obligatory practices.[2]

The rise of Christianity in the Roman Empire led to a distinctively Christian adaptation of the concept of religion. The influential theologian St. Augustine expanded on this in a short book entirely devoted to the subject, *Of True Religion* (390 C.E.). This was in part a philosophical treatise in which Augustine argued that true religion meant acknowledging the creator with reverence, uniting a correct intellectual perspective with appropriate attitudes and actions. The exact nature of this acknowledgment could vary from one age to another. Augustine felt that in earlier times the non-Christian philosopher Plato had been an example of true religion. In the fourth century C.E. he announced the divine arrangement or dispensation for humanity was Christianity, uniting the philosophy of Plato with the truth of Christ. Augustine went on to articulate a detailed series of intellectual and spiritual stages of development that were available to the seekers of true religion. Several points emerged, however, as radical innovations in this Christian concept of religion. First, for Augustine, true religion only existed in the singular; he did not have any concept of multiple religions. Second, religion was now a subject that had strong theological and doctrinal content. Third, the source of authority for the articulation of proper attitudes and actions was located in the Christian Church, as the historic tradition connecting humanity with Christ; religion was not merely an abstract teaching but depended on revelation expressed in time and space, in a historical and local context. Uniting theological truth with the legal authority of the church would have immense repercussions for the development of Christianity.

A major shift in the concept of religion can be detected at the dawn of the modern era, some fourteen centuries later. Major and drastic transformations had taken place in European Christianity since the time of Augustine, not the least of which was the split caused by the Protestant Reformation. A convenient example of the new perspective can be seen in the work of the famous Dutch jurist Hugo Grotius in his book *On the Truth of the Christian Religion* (published in Latin in 1627). Although the title appears superficially similar to that of Augustine's book, the difference is profound. Particularly in the wake of the European wars of religion between Protestant and Catholic, it had become clear that religion is a noun in the plural — there are multiple religions that all claim the same authority. Glossing over the split within Christianity, Grotius turned his gaze outward and described non-Christian groups as religions, too, although necessarily false ones.

Grotius's book, in fact, was a debating manual for European sailors on missions of economic and military conquest; it was designed to help them convert the Jew, the Muslim, and the pagan to Christianity. What is new about this perspective? As with Augustine, doctrinal truth and legal authority are claimed for Christianity. But now Christianity is only one of several religions that are in competition for world domination. The framework for this new emphasis was the era of European colonialism, which can be dated back to the time of Columbus but began to hit its full stride by the end of the eighteenth century.

It is worth pausing to examine the picture of religion that emerges from the extremely popular work of Grotius (it was translated into multiple languages, and the Latin version was a standard school text through the mid-1800s in England). If one looks at the frontispiece of the English translation published in 1632 (*True Religion Explained and Defended against ye Archenemies Thereof in These Times*), one sees a portrait of religion as an allegorical female figure poised between the New Testament and the Old Testament (fig. 2.1). In separate portraits around the page, the Christian is contrasted with the Jew, the Muslim (here called "the Turke"), and the pagan, each with a suitable biblical verse describing their relative status. Notes to the frontispiece explain the basic concept of Islam as both violent and false: "The Turke stands with his sword in his hand, by which he defends his Religion, that sprang from Mahomet (Muhammad), a false Prophet, foretold in generall by Christ." Without going into all the details, one can see here in the overall trend from "religion" to "religions" a concept of competing beliefs and political communities in a context of imperialism and missions. Grotius's conclusion to this book is as follows: "There is not, neither ever was there any other Religion in the whole world [other than Christianity], that can bee imagined more honourable for excellency of reward, more absolute and perfect for precepts, or more admirable for the manner according to which it was commanded to bee propagated and divulged."[3] This unsurprising choice of Christianity as the supreme religion of the world and the automatic assumption of the falsity of other religions is another aspect of the modern European concept of religion. All this will have particular importance for the concept of Islam.

In setting up this global conflict between Christianity and all other religions, Grotius skips a crucial conflict internal to Christianity, which has had immense repercussions for the modern

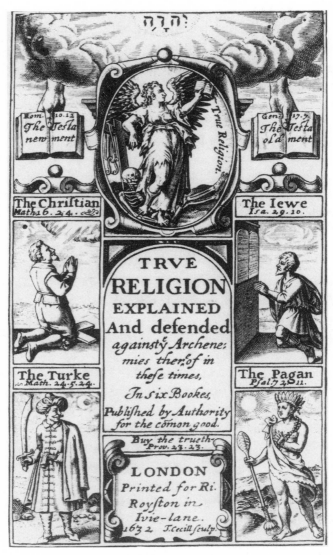

FIGURE 2.1

Frontispiece of True Religion Explained and Defended against ye Archenemies Thereof in These Times, *by Hugo Grotius (London, 1632)*

concept of religion. The Protestant Reformation was arguably the biggest crisis in the history of Christianity. It led to immense social upheavals, including peasant revolts, apocalyptic uprisings, and interminable wars between Protestant and Catholic, based on religious identity. Politics was so closely fused with religion that the slogan of the day was "religion belongs to the ruler" (*cuius regio eius religio*); that is, the state religion would be dictated by the ruler. These bloody and prolonged religious wars eventually provoked revulsion against intolerance of different religious beliefs. A series of philosophers and thinkers began to advocate that morality and behavior alone should be controlled by the state, while belief could remain a private matter. The culmination of this doctrine of the Enlightenment came in the concept of freedom of religion and tolerance, as seen in the rejection of established state religion by the framers of the American Constitution. But many European countries (with the exception of revolutionary France and various Communist regimes) have continued to accept various forms of official state recognition of particular churches. Still, in general terms, this shift to modernity has decisively elevated the power of the state over religion in matters of law and political authority while leaving various religious groups in competition in the realm of belief. In the colonies, however, with their large numbers of non-Christian subjects, Christian missionaries were given free rein and encouragement to seek new converts. The essential point to be noted is that religious toleration in Europe was only extended to different varieties of Christianity; non-Christian religions did not receive this concession.

Since the terms of debate about religion have been set by the modern colonial era, it is not surprising that Muslims (along with other non-Christians) have responded by defending themselves in the same language. Some major changes in modern Muslim thinking about religion are outlined below. The intense preoccupation of Christians with missionary activity, particularly in the last few centuries, has no equivalent in Islamic history before modern times. Yet Christians, in what psychologists might call a form of projection, have constructed a highly simplified and misleading picture of Islam as fueled by a relentless thirst to convert the world—preferably at the edge of the sword. The serious distortions in this picture will be discussed later in this book, but ironically, the missionary concept of Islam has been picked up enthusiastically by many modern Muslims. The general mentality associated with missions generates similar questions and concepts. For instance, Christians and Muslims are equally likely to discuss with gusto the question of which religion is superior. Everyone is equipped with arguments to prove that his or her religion is supreme, and a practically endless series of examples could be given to demonstrate this. Yet the assumptions of this imperialistic missionary attitude about the nature of religion are rarely examined. Even nonreligious people examining an unfamiliar religion for the first time feel as though they are being called upon either to accept or to reject the religion in terms of personal allegiance.

The postmodern and postcolonial world, however, calls for a different approach to religion. Except for the diehard fanatics who are intent on converting the world to their doctrine, it should be apparent to everyone that religious pluralism is a fact of life. Not only do we have to accept the existence of multiple religions, but we must also acknowledge the nonreligious option as a significant and legitimate choice. In pluralistic modern societies, to assert the authority of a particular holy book, according to a particular "literal" interpretation, amounts to a tyrannical assertion of power. Although this is precisely what religious fundamentalists do, in practice they can only attain this authority by suppressing or eliminating everyone who holds a different point of view.

Interestingly, the Islamic tradition possesses extensive resources that lend themselves to concepts of religious pluralism. The Qur'an (2:256) explicitly states, "There is no compulsion in religion." Religious dogma plays a much smaller role for Muslims than it does for Christians, who in various periods of history have been much more absorbed with questions of orthodoxy and heresy. Modern Christianity tends to be viewed primarily in terms of belief, whereas Muslims (like Jews) have generally emphasized legal and ethical practice more than theology and doctrine. Among the large majority of Sunni Muslims, the four principal schools of law are equally acceptable. A well-known statement of the Prophet Muhammad illustrates this concept of pluralism and is often understood as authorizing different interpretations of Islamic law: "Difference of opinion is a mercy for my community." It would be hard to find the equivalent to this recognition of pluralism in any Christian theological doctrine.

With respect to other religions, Islamic thinkers have traditionally accepted the concept of multiple revelations, in the concept of the "peoples of the book." The Qur'an invokes the authority of the prophets Abraham, Moses, Jesus, and many others, some of whose names are central to the texts of the Bible. Three major earlier scriptures are cited in the Qur'an: the Torah of Moses, the Psalms of David, and the Gospel of Jesus. And there were certainly indications that there may have been many other prophets who brought revelations. The Qur'an depicts this multiplicity as part of the divine plan: "For everyone we have established a law, and a way. If God had wished, he would have made you a single community, but this was so he might test you regarding what he sent you. So try to be first in doing what is best" (5:48). Thus Islamic law contained a legal category for protected religious minorities, defined mainly with respect to Jews and Christians but extended in practice to other groups such as Zoroastrians and Hindus. This legal status guaranteed these communities protection for their lives and property and for the practice of their religion; they were exempted from military service but were required to pay additional taxes. In practice, there have been instances in which particular Muslim rulers persecuted religious minorities. But it is important to acknowledge the existence of legal principles protecting religious minorities in Muslim societies. This stands in contrast to Christian Europe, where non-Christian minorities had no legal rights whatever but were entirely dependent on the goodwill of the political authorities. It was for this reason that Jewish communities in Europe were so vulnerable to persecution during the Christian Middle Ages.

Non-Muslim commentators, who often take modern extremist Muslims to be the only true Muslims, frequently characterize Islam as an intolerant religion. Yet religious pluralism was built into the social structure of most premodern Muslim societies, insofar as they observed the principles established in Islamic law. Indeed, it is surprising that while Christian authorities eradicated paganism in Europe centuries ago, pre-Islamic pagan groups still exist in some Muslim countries. The Mandaean community, an ancient non-Christian religious group that reveres John the Baptist, is based in Iraq and Iran and has perhaps 45,000 members worldwide. In the upper Himalayan region of Chitral in Pakistan, about 3,000 members of the Kalash trace their descent from the soldiers of Alexander the Great and practice a polytheistic religion. Unlike Christian Europe, Muslim societies had no equivalent of the Inquisition to implement a systematic policy of repression of religious minorities.

How have traditional Muslim doctrines of pluralism played out in recent times? The dissolution of premodern Muslim societies and the establishment of colonial rule have led to novel transformations in the role of religion and law. The premodern societies ruled by Muslims generally cannot, in fact, be called Islamic in any fundamental sense. Politically speaking, within a generation after the death of the Prophet Muhammad (632 C.E.), the Arabs established an empire modeled on the world-imperial domains of the Persians and the Romans. Later dynasties ruled in the style of Persian kingship or emulated the Central Asian empire of Genghis Khan. While Islamic law and symbolism played important roles within these empires, they were always accompanied by a combination of traditional local custom and administrative edict, neither of which derives from Islamic religious sources. Only in the twentieth century was a new kind of Islamic ideology created, in which life in its totality would be lived exclusively according to Islam. This modern concept of the Islamic state has a powerful emotional appeal, but it is paradoxical. While it attempts to bypass the preceding fourteen centuries of history and re-create the ideal religious society established by the Prophet Muhammad, it does so through the apparatus of the modern bureaucratic postcolonial state. So, like any other nation-state, contemporary Muslim societies define religion and the status of minorities through constitutions and legal codes that differ considerably from the legal and religious structures of the past. Since the theorists of the modern Islamic state are responding to European colonialism, the modern concept of religion has had a powerful influence in refashioning the concept of Islam.

Islam and the Historical Study of Religion

While the modern study of religion originated within Catholic and Protestant academic circles, it has grown to encompass a bewildering array of religious traditions from around the world.

Many attempts have been made to come up with systems of classification, although it was common to use Christianity as a template and to assume that other religions had the same basic features (scripture, priesthood, theology, and ritual), merely substituting different content in each case. In practice, however, it is difficult to make clear analogies between familiar Christian phenomena and other traditions. In addition, one can scarcely overestimate the importance of Christian missionary activity, particularly during the height of European colonialism in the nineteenth century, as a factor in the understanding of non-Christian religions. This missionary background, which assumes an imperial contest among religions for world domination, is evident in some of the main concepts used to understand religion on a global scale.

One of these familiar concepts of religion is comparative religion, an idea that in part arose in Protestant seminaries to answer the question, Which religion is better? In a missionary context, such comparisons usually juxtaposed one's own ideal with another's less than perfect practice, an approach that could be handy in debates with potential converts. Since the early twentieth century, the idea of comparative religion has shifted into a less missionary and more theoretical attempt to understand common structures that may be found in many traditions. Another popular concept, world religions (usually contrasted with folk or local religions), explicitly classified certain religions as competitive missionary religions on a global scale, awarding a major significance to large population figures. Again, this concept implicitly accepts the European colonial attempt at world domination as the context for understanding multiple religions. Usually Christianity, Islam, and Buddhism qualified as the main contenders for the status of missionary world religions, and everything else was considered local. Since Islam and Christianity both have significantly larger numbers of followers than does

Buddhism, this concept set the stage for a serious confrontation between Christians and Muslims.

The categorization of religions is an incredibly difficult task. The earliest efforts proceeded along the lines of the famous classification systems of Linnaean biology, strangely enough. The basic assumption was that there were certain broad major categories, similar to the genus of biology, that could then be broken down into species and subspecies. This biological method, derived from comparative zoology, is another source of the use of the term "comparative" in the phrase "comparative religion." One of the main problems with treating religious traditions as biological species is that competing groups claim the mantle of legitimacy and reject the claims of others. This means that there are multiple sources of order within each religion that challenge one another (think, for instance, of the evangelical and fundamentalist Christian groups who regard the Catholic Church as a corruption and betrayal of true Christianity or even consider the pope to be the Antichrist). Further, the biological model of distinguishing characteristics of a species fails miserably when it comes to describing religious groups. Some, for instance, would define Christianity as belief in the divinity of Jesus Christ, but this definition collides with self-described Christians (such as the Arian movement in antiquity or Unitarians today) who do not regard Jesus as divine. Likewise, definitions of Judaism, whether by practices such as circumcision or in terms of belief, run up against cases that confound standard expectations, such as the Messianic Jews or "Jews for Jesus." The definition of Islam runs into similar difficulties, both with established sectarian movements (such as various branches of Shiʻism) and with modern ideological groups (like the Taliban).

Scholars of religious studies in North American universities in recent decades have tried to focus on historical understanding and interpretation instead of doctrinal authority and political competition. If this way of studying religion has an aim that differs from that of missionary and colonial concepts of religion, it is to permit a notion of pluralistic community based on mutual understanding, rather than assuming that one imposes an authoritarian religious doctrine. The peculiarly American notion of separation of church and state is probably a factor in this concept of pluralism. Although there are some who would still try to claim that the United States is or should be a Christian nation, there have been numerous court decisions making it plain that the Constitution does not permit endorsing one particular religious perspective over others. On the other hand, there has also been a recognition of the importance of religion for understanding our complicated history and culture. As Justice Arthur Goldberg observed, "The Court would recognize the propriety . . . of the teaching about religion, as distinguished from the teaching of religion, in the public schools."[4] The important distinction here is between teaching *about* religion, which is an academic study, and the teaching *of* religion, which is the inculcation of doctrine and the training for practice appropriate to religious communities. It is perhaps because of this distinctive historical experience that academic departments of religion, unattached to particular churches or theologies, are found in hundreds of colleges and universities throughout North America. In contrast, teaching about religion as a separate subject outside theological seminaries is comparatively rare in Europe, Asia, and Africa.

One of the important insights that have emerged from the study of religion as a historical and cultural reality is the realization that religions change; they are not timeless, eternal essences. There are, moreover, major divisions within all of the large abstract categories that we typically find in the common lists of world religions. A prominent example of this historical approach is the work of the late Wilfred Cantwell Smith, who argued forcefully that "religion" is an ambiguous term that has to be broken down into two major components. The first is what may be called religious experience or faith, which is the internal dimension of religion and is of immediate concern to religious practitioners and professionals. The second component of religion is what Smith calls the cumulative tradition, the external dimension, which includes scriptures, ritual practice, morality, law, literature and myth, knowledge of the natural world, art and architecture, teaching or doctrine, family and community, the political order, and the like. This external aspect of religion may be observed by anyone, regardless of religious background or faith commitment. The cumulative tradition of religion grows and changes throughout history, and this can be documented, explained, debated, and interpreted; but this tradition is in theory accessible to everyone, whether they belong to the religion in question or not.

A major consequence of the historical study of religion is that it becomes increasingly impossible to consider a religion to be a "thing" (scholars called this process the "objectification" or "reification" of religion).[5] Although it is common to hear people say, for example, "Christianity says that . . . " or "according to Islam . . . ," the only thing that can be observed or demonstrated is that individual people who call themselves Christians or Muslims have particular positions and practices that they observe and defend. No one, however, has ever seen Christianity or Islam do anything. They are abstractions, not actors comparable to human beings. Moreover, the atmosphere of contest between different religions has given rise to a subtle but momentous shift of perspective in which people speak of believing in Christianity or in Islam, as opposed to believing in God. Again, as Smith pointed out, there is something almost idolatrous about putting a religion into the place of God, given the very human history of all religions. But in the popular media and in modern discourse about religions, it is common to treat them as if they were things that could be compared and contrasted according to their essences.

Unlike Smith, however, I do not privilege the internal dimension of faith or religious experience as something beyond historical conditions, restricted only to the believer. Nevertheless, Smith's emphasis on religious tradition as historical is an important insight that has seriously eroded the concept of religions as having essential characteristics, at least in the academic study of religion. As Smith himself pointed out, if religion is part of history, then we have to take seriously the point that history (with all of its changes and transformations) has no essence. Thus a classical definition of religion in general, or of any particular religion, would be contradictory, since any such definition presupposes an unchanging essence. I therefore use "religion" and "religions" in a contextual and provisional fashion, qualifying the terms as much as possible with particular historical circumstances to illuminate the issue at hand.[6]

From a parallel perspective, the study of religion can be broken down into prescriptive and descriptive approaches. Religious communities define their faith and practice in an authoritative fashion, judging what is appropriate and inappropriate from their perspective. It is up to them to prescribe the authentic or true way to follow their teachings. It is not the duty of outsiders who may be interested in a particular religious tradition to make these prescriptive decisions. Instead, they have the ability to describe what has taken place in the history of that tradition, and most would agree that the ethics of scholarship requires these descriptions to be fair-minded and respectful, and that they should in some measure take account of the views of practitioners of that religion. But in the many instances where there are deep disagreements within a religious tradition, outside scholars and commentators have a limited role. It would be inappropriate, for instance, for a Hindu scholar to take sides on the issues of the Protestant Reformation—to decide, for instance, that either the pope or Martin Luther was correct. While particular Christian communities may find it necessary to take sides on this dispute, it is absurd for someone who has no stake in the matter to attempt to decide which is the authoritative interpretation; that would be a prescriptive rather than a descriptive move, and a misguided one at that. What is appropriate for the scholar is to explain what was at stake in this momentous conflict. By explaining the significance and importance of the arguments and the actors, the scholar is able to illuminate the history of religion in a way that both insiders and outsiders should be able to appreciate.

It is important to clarify the difference between the internal and external aspects of religion, between religious experience and the cumulative tradition, and between the prescriptive and descriptive approaches to religion, because they are often confused. It is particularly important for those who wish to understand Islam, because uninformed commentators—mostly from the news media—have been the principal sources of information for the general public. These media sources, whose role in depicting religion will be discussed at greater length later, are for the most part willing to relay the most extreme religious positions without attempting to put them into context or to relate them to majority views. Some reporters even appear to provoke extreme statements, since these will have greater impact on the evening news. When a religious extremist tells a television reporter that Islam requires holy war against the infidel West, this prescriptive minority view of Islam suddenly acquires an authority from the media that it could never attain within its own social context. In the absence of reliable descriptive information about Islam in the public sphere of Western countries, it is now vitally important to explain and distinguish between the many voices that speak in the name of Islam.

Several other important conclusions follow from this historical approach to religion. If beliefs and practices change over time, and if interpretations are subject to change as well, then what is the role of sacred scriptures? Here the answer must be that the importance and the understanding of holy books vary from one religious tradition to another and can vary a great deal within a particular tradition. The Protestant approach to religion has supplied the most common model of the role of scripture. Protestant Christians, after all, distinguished themselves from Catholics by using the slogan "scripture alone" (*sola scriptura*, in Latin), whereas the Catholics insisted on the additional importance of Church tradition as equally authoritative alongside scripture. In addition, religious specialists have most often interpreted holy books according to a large and complex body of commentaries. The Protestant notion of "the priesthood of the believer," with every individual able to approach scripture independently, unencumbered by the accumulated traditions of religious knowledge, has few parallels in the history of other religions.

This Protestant model of religion lay behind early attempts to study non-Christian religions, as shown in such examples as the famous *Sacred Books of the East* series edited by F. Max Müller in the late nineteenth century. The problem was that most other religious traditions did not have a single compact body of scriptures similar to the Bible; in some cases, there are dozens or even hundreds of holy books of more or less relevance to major numbers of believers. A good example would be Buddhism, where one can find three vast and only partially overlapping major sets of scriptures, each in a different language (Tibetan, Chinese, and Pali). But the focus of many mod-

ern Protestant denominations on the Bible has led to the expectation that one can understand everything of importance of the
other religious traditions if one knows what is said in their
scriptures. This concept of scripturalism is tempting, but it is a
fallacy. It assumes that all scriptural verses are equally weighty,
that there is no debate about their meaning, and that there has
been no change over the centuries in the understanding of particular verses. It also assumes that every member of a particular
religious group is equally certain to follow every prescription
found in the holy book (or books). Can one predict the behavior of a Christian simply by taking a verse out of the Bible and
assuming that it has a controlling influence over that person? In
reality, one would need to know a good deal more before making such a prediction.

Another important conclusion is the difficulty of evaluating
adherence to a particular religion. How does one define a Christian? The results will vary dramatically depending on the yard-
stick one uses. If religion is defined by belief, the number of
Christians will probably be much higher than if it is defined by
practice. And if belief is the norm, how does one deal with
smaller groups who differ significantly from the mainstream in
what they believe? I have had students ask me in all seriousness
whether Catholics are really Christians. From the viewpoint of
some Christian communities, Catholics may appear to be outside the pale of Christianity, and the reverse may be true as well.
What about groups such as Mormons, Jehovah's Witnesses, or
the Unification Church, who consider themselves Christians
but are regarded with ambivalence by others? If one follows the
prescriptive view of religion and defines Christianity from, say,
the Baptist perspective, the definition of membership in the
mainstream of religion will exclude significant numbers of people because they do not have the correct beliefs. This kind of
definition will also leave unexplained the fact that the excluded

people still consider themselves Christians. For this reason, most scholars follow the descriptive method, and they accept instead the self-identification of people as the only way to describe religious membership meaningfully. This is a sociological rather than a theological approach to religious identity.[7] There are admittedly many cases where it is quite difficult to establish consistent judgments about religious identity (the Nation of Islam, for instance, poses such a problem with respect to its Islamic identity). But this difficulty in categorizing and defining religion seems to be unavoidable.[8]

Despite the efforts of scholars, the level of knowledge about Islam is quite low among the general public, even among those who consider themselves well educated. Partly this is because the study of Islam has been carried out by specialists in academic departments of Near Eastern studies, who perpetuate a tradition of detailed academic study of past civilizations, which is often opaque and inaccessible to nonspecialists. In the more modern centers of Middle Eastern studies, funded by the federal government to aid policy users, the tendency is to focus on contemporary political issues at the expense of long-term cultural and humanistic subjects. In North America, while the growth of the study of religions besides Christianity expanded considerably in the 1960s, the study of Islam has lagged behind other fields. Currently there are barely 200 active scholars in North America who identify themselves as specialists in Islamic studies, though there are somewhat larger numbers of specialists in Middle Eastern history and politics. These scholars have contributed many significant and insightful studies of Muslim societies and cultures through their publications. Unfortunately, much of this information is not accessible to the general public, either because it is located in hard-to-find academic journals or, in the case of university press publications, because it is too often produced in limited quantities and aimed primarily at other scholars. This knowledge about Islam could be much more relevant and helpful to a wider public if it were expressed in a more accessible fashion, without specialist jargon. At the same time, it should be recognized that the reading public sometimes is looking for authoritative pronouncements about the truth of religion rather than informative descriptions. The task for contemporary society is to come up with a way of speaking civilly about religion without staking authoritative claims that exclude certain parties from the conversation. The academic study of religion offers tools that can help create a new civil discourse about Islam.

Islam Defined by the State and by the Numbers

Defining religious identity is not just a theoretical problem, however. In practice, religion is defined by the state, throughout the world. In the United States, the Internal Revenue Service (IRS), the Immigration and Naturalization Service (INS), and the courts are the primary definers of religion. Since the U.S. tax code exempts religious groups from taxation, is up to the IRS to decide whether a particular religion is legitimate or fraudulent. Likewise, the INS awards visas for immigrant religious teachers on the basis of its determination of their authenticity. Of course the courts have the responsibility of interpreting religion in relation to the Constitution, deciding, for instance, whether the teaching of creationism in the public schools constitutes an establishment of religion by the state. The situation is similar in other countries. States such as Germany have ruled that the Church of Scientology is not a legitimate religion. Israel, following the legal precedent of Ottoman law, defines membership in religions strictly according to the community into which one was born. Therefore, in Israel it does not matter if one converts to another religion or joins a Hare Krishna group; one still can only be married and buried according to one's original birth religion as defined by the state.

The possible disconnect between religious belief and religious identity is nicely illustrated by a story about a student who was filling in a registration form at the American University in Beirut. When he left the space marked "religion" blank, the student was told that the registration form was incomplete and that he had to specify his religion. "But I'm an atheist!" he protested. Patiently, the registrar asked, "Yes, but are you a Christian atheist, a Jewish atheist, or a Muslim atheist?" The key question here is not religious belief but membership in a politically identifiable community. That is how states tend to define religion.

For these reasons, statistics and census figures on religion should be viewed with great caution. The overall categories are subject to debate, and the qualifications for membership vary considerably. Some of the first attempts to conduct a census on religion were carried out by the British colonial government in India in 1881, when a massive survey of practically every village in the subcontinent required respondents to indicate their religious affiliation (among many other items). This was in many cases the first time these people had been asked what their religion was, and certainly it was the first time they were offered only one choice. The British administrators assumed that, as with political parties, it is possible to belong to only one religion at a time. But in India it has been common practice for centuries for people to attend multiple religious shrines, perhaps on the basis of a practical impulse to maximize the possibility of divine protection. Thus it is common for Hindus, Christians, Sikhs, and Muslims to pay their respects at the same religious sites, although the practices and beliefs of the different communities may vary. Likewise, a survey of religious identity carried out in Japan in the 1960s offered respondents as many as four categories from which to choose their affiliation, including Buddhist, Shinto, Confucian, and Christian. To the surprise of the survey takers, most respondents checked two boxes, and some checked three. Deciding on one's religious identity was apparently not as simple as the American researchers had assumed. Not only can religious practice be more complicated than simple affiliation, but there may be practical economic and political consequences to the declaration of a particular religious identity. At the time of the first British censuses in India, some groups wondered whether to declare themselves as Hindus or to seek a separate identity, and uppermost in their minds were the tax implications of either choice. Similarly, one finds a tendency to inflate or minimize census figures when the political importance of particular religious groups is in question. Census figures on religion, then, are statistical classifications of groups rather than guides to belief or behavior.

Keeping these cautions in mind, it is useful to look at the most commonly cited census figures relative to Islam. It is clear that the world Muslim population is second only to the Christian population among major religious communities. The current total Muslim population, including all sectarian divisions, is thought to be about 1.3 billion, or roughly one of every four or five people alive today. The comparable figure for all branches of Christianity is roughly 1.8 billion people, although these numbers are quite general and estimates vary considerably. In terms of major sectarian divisions, it is thought that from 10 to 15 percent of Muslims are Shi'is (Shi'ites), while the remaining majority are loosely classified as Sunni. These two large categories obscure other important distinctions, such as the four major schools of Islamic law recognized by Sunnis, as well as the theological positions associated with particular modern religious academies and movements (these categories will be discussed in more detail later).

Just as important as these overall religious figures, and perhaps more revealing, are the numbers for ethnic identity and national identity. Contrary to the common stereotype, Arabs are far from being a majority of Muslims. Although there are around 250 million Arabs (some of whom are Christians) in twenty different countries, Arabs comprise roughly 18 percent of the world Muslim population. Probably the next biggest ethnic group of Muslims is the Bengalis, with about 200 million people mostly split between Bangladesh and India. The nations with the greatest Muslim populations are in the East, the largest being Indonesia (180 million), Pakistan (150 million), Bangladesh (130 million), and India (120 million). Thus half of the Muslim population lives east of Karachi, in environments more often characterized by tropical climate and rice farming than by the deserts associated with Arab countries. The next largest Muslim populations are in Egypt, Iran, Turkey, and Nigeria, with around 60 million Muslims each. Despite its economic and political prominence, Saudi Arabia has only about 15 million people. All in all, more than fifty countries have a Muslim majority, but the role that Islamic religious authority plays in each case is different.

The situation is quite different in countries where Muslims form a minority. Sometimes, as in the case of China, Muslims have been longtime residents of particular regions, although the total Chinese Muslim population is only about 30 million according to the most reliable estimates. But immigration to Europe and the Americas has created new living situations for Muslims. The U.S. Muslim population has been variously estimated to be between 3 million and 7 million, although most observers would probably settle around 5 million, placing American Muslims in a position comparable to that of the Mormons or Lutherans in terms of population; there are probably more Muslims than Jews in the United States. In terms of origins, American Muslims may be conveniently divided into two groups that are roughly equal in size. Most immigrant Muslims have arrived in the United States since the liberalization of immigration laws in the 1960s. The largest segment of immigrant Muslims, about 45 percent, derives from South Asia (primarily India and Pakistan). Other major sources of Muslim immigration are Iran and various Arab countries, although the vast majority of Arab Americans (about 90 percent) are Christians. It must be emphasized that the religious attitudes of American Muslims are not uniform, for they include sectarian as well as relatively secular tendencies. Many local mosques cater to a particular ethnic or national group, although larger cities have cosmopolitan mosques frequented by people from different countries.

The other major group of American Muslims is from the African American community, with probably 2.5 million in all. This African American Islamic identity is based primarily on conversions since the 1930s, but it reflects a deeper historical reality; up to 15 percent of the Africans who were enslaved and sent to North America were Muslims. The greatest amount of publicity for any American Muslim movement undoubtedly attaches to the Nation of Islam, because of its controversial involvement with racial theories of black supremacy. A confrontational attitude against white society and a highly unusual theology have characterized the Nation of Islam from its early period under Elijah Mohammed and Malcolm X to Louis Farrakhan today. It should be pointed out, however, that the vast majority of African American Muslims left the Nation of Islam in the late 1970s under the leadership of Imam Wallace D. Mohammed (son of Elijah Mohammed), who renounced the racial doctrines of that movement. Thus while at least 2 million African American Muslims follow norms of Islamic practice that would be recognizable by Muslims anywhere in the world, the tiny Nation of Islam probably has no more than 25,000 members today. The disproportionately high profile of the Nation of Islam is a direct product of the news media and their obsession with conflict. There is also a small but significant number of Euro-American converts to Islam.

In Europe the Muslim population is around 10 million, with large concentrations in England, France, and Germany resulting from immigration in recent decades. There is considerable diversity among the European Muslim population as well. This results not only from differing national origins (Indians and Pakistanis in England, Algerians in France, and Turks in Germany) but also from a lot of variation on a spectrum that covers traditional conservatism, fundamentalism, and outright secularism. With demographic patterns and immigration expected to continue and increase, it is likely that the Muslim populations of European and American countries will likewise expand over the coming decades.

Islamic Religious Language

Because the Islamic tradition is so poorly understood in America and Europe, it is important to establish some basic terms that are used both to describe the religion from without and to elaborate on it from within. To begin with, the term "Islam" (with stress on the second syllable, which is a long vowel) comes from an Arabic word meaning "submission," with the implication of submission to God; it is also related to the Arabic word *salam*, meaning peace. A person who submits to God is called a Muslim (this spelling is preferable to the older form, Moslem).

The word "Muslim" should be pronounced without turning the *s* into a *z*, as English speakers tend to do; that mispronunciation unfortunately resembles the Arabic word *muzlim*, which means tyrant. Today we tend to use the word "Islam" as the name of a religion, in the specifically modern sense described above; in this sense, it is parallel with the word "Christianity." Likewise, a Muslim is a person who is an adherent to the religion of Islam, much as the Christian adheres to Christianity. It is also common for people to speak of Islam in a normative or prescriptive sense, referring to some kind of authoritative ideal of how things should be, while the term "Muslim" has a sense of the historical actuality of what people have done in practice. That is the ordinary usage.

The Arabic term *islam* itself was of relatively minor importance in classical theologies based on the Qur'an. If one looks at the works of theologians such as the famous al-Ghazali (d. 1111), the key term of religious identity is not *islam* but *iman*, or faith, and the one who possesses it is the *mu'min*, or believer. Faith is one of the major topics of the Qur'an; it is mentioned hundreds of times in the sacred text. In comparison, *islam* is a relatively less common term of secondary importance; it only occurs eight times in the Qur'an. Since, however, the term *islam* had a derivative meaning relating to the community of those who have submitted to God, it has taken on a new political significance, especially in recent history. Surprisingly, in eastern or non-Arab countries, followers of the faith were not typically known by the Arabic term *muslim* until relatively recent years, when in places such as India the Arabic usage has come to be consciously preferred. Instead, they were called *musalman*, a term evidently related to *muslim* but which by its irregular form suggests a non-Arab identity.[9]

Among the collected sayings of the Prophet Muhammad (known as *hadith* in Arabic), one famous account depicts a meeting between Muhammad and an enigmatic figure identified as the angel Gabriel. This stranger asked the Prophet to describe three concepts that are fundamental to Islamic religious thought. The first was submission to God (*islam*), which the Prophet described as the performance of five basic acts: professing faith in God and in the Prophet, performing ritual prayer, fasting during the month of Ramadan, giving alms to the poor, and going on pilgrimage to Mecca, provided one has the means. Since most of these activities are carried out in the community, *islam* in this sense has a strong social compónent. The second concept was faith (*iman*), which Muhammad explained in terms of having faith in God, the prophets, the angels, the holy books, the Day of Judgment, and God's foreknowledge or predestination. The third term was spiritual virtue (*ihsan*), meaning that you pray as though you see God face-to-face, for even though you do not see God, you must know that God sees you. This striking dialogue (Gabriel expressed his approval of Muhammad's responses) indicates a structure of religious values that proceeds from the outer to the inner. Submission (*islam*) is the first and most external step, while the next two steps, faith and spiritual virtue, are affairs of the mind and heart, creating the basis for religious consciousness. To the extent that current interpretations of Islam exclude the internal aspects of faith and spiritual virtue, they present an impoverished picture of this religious tradition.[10]

In this book, I try to avoid referring to Islam as a changeless monolithic religion that somehow homogenizes hundreds of millions of people from different times and places. I use "Islamic" to refer to an orientation in which the primary scriptural focus is the Qur'an and the leading personal model is the Prophet Muhammad, without insisting on any particular authoritative structure beyond this simple formulation. Following Marshall Hodgson, I use "Islamicate" to describe civilizational and cultural practices accepted by Muslims and non-Muslims alike, which are associated with Islamic religious tradition but which do not themselves derive from the primary Islamic scriptural sources.[11] Thus we can speak of Islamicate art or literature as cultural products that do not necessarily have any specifically religious origin but that flourished in situations where Islam was a dominant element.

If the European concept of religion has changed over the centuries, and if it only imperfectly fits other religious traditions, then what would be the parallel concepts that emerge from indigenous Islamic sources? Here we need to enter the complex and allusive religious vocabulary of classical Arabic, which is founded in the primary sacred text, the Qur'an, but which has been elaborated on by religious thinkers over the centuries. Just to take one important example, the Arabic word most often used as an equivalent for "religion" is *din*, which has no plural in the Qur'an. The root meaning of *din* carries the senses of judgment, debt, obligation, custom, and guidance that is accepted with submission. Sometimes one of these senses dominates the others, as in the common Arabic expression for Day of Judgment (*din*). While it resembles the Latin *religio* in the sense of obligation and duty, *din* differs from the Christian concept of religion in that it originates in the will of God rather than being primarily a human allegiance. Frequently the Qur'an identifies this as the "religion of Abraham" (*din Ibrahim*), connecting with the ancient prophet, or the "religion of truth" (*din al-haqq*) deriving directly from God. Muhammad's response to Gabriel articulating the threefold elements of submission to God, faith, and spiritual virtue is sometimes described as the definition of *din*. Religion as *din* was often contrasted with the material world, or *dunya*, although the Islamic religious perspective always put ethical demands on society.

The points just mentioned served as the basis for centuries of reflection and debate in matters of theology, law, and related fields. I will not attempt to summarize here all of the different points of view that developed in Islamic history. It is important, however, to call attention to a series of dramatic new developments that took place just more than a century ago in Muslim countries, in part in response to European colonialism. These movements are often called reformist, and many of them can be traced to thinkers such as the Iranian philosopher Jamal al-Din Afghani (d. 1897) and his Egyptian follower Muhammad Abduh (d. 1905). They also drew upon the relentless puritanical movement of the Wahhabis, who had been active in the Arabian Peninsula since the end of the eighteenth century. The reformers presented themselves as correcting and restoring religion to its original purity. Their preferred name for themselves was the Salafiyya, a term taken from the pious forefathers, that is, the first few generations of Muslims. Despite the rhetoric of returning to the ancient golden age under the Prophet Muhammad, this movement originated in the shadow of modern European empires and their growing influence in regions such as the Arabic provinces of the Ottoman empire. They were profoundly impressed by the techniques and dedication of Christian missionaries, particularly the Protestants, and they were quick to adopt modern technologies of mass communication such as printing. Salafi and Wahhabi thinking has evolved into a rigid and authoritarian minority view that regards much of Muslim civilization and history as anathema to their concept of pure Islam.[12]

Modern Islamic reform movements are very much a part of contemporary history. Their insistence on recovering the original uncorrupted purity of the faith and their adherence to scripture to the exclusion of all later additions have an eerie and remarkable similarity to the Protestant Christian ethos. Perhaps for this reason, Americans and Europeans from largely Protestant countries have been tempted to accept at face value the reformist's claim to represent "true Islam." British colonial administrators in their friendlier moments complimented Islam as being a religion without priests, with simple doctrines that did not require abstruse theology—in other words, for being similar to Protestantism. Condescending Euro-American commentators sometimes remark that what Islam needs today is a Reformation—in other words, that Islam needs to undergo the kind of revolution that occurred in Protestant Europe, in the process dethroning the authority of tradition. What these patronizing observers fail to realize is that the Protestant Reformation has already occurred in Islam. The continuing export of fire-breathing Christian missionaries to Muslim countries provided a new example of how one can use the authority of scripture to bash one's opponents. The recent practitioners of this art, who belong to Muslim reformist and fundamentalist camps, are typically self-taught experts who have avoided traditional Islamic education; indeed, they consider the traditional Muslim academies to be largely irrelevant. The exclusivist zeal of the Protestant Reformation has called forth a mirror image among Muslim reformists, and the similarity of names is not accidental.

The impact of Christian ideas of religion has also drawn negative responses, however. A comment often heard in Muslim reformist circles is "Islam is not a religion, but a way of life." Implicit in this remark is a critique of the current European and American notion of religion as an essentially private affair that has no authority over public space. To introduce another modern term, the reformist thinking that aims at transforming society can be seen as a form of ideology. A dramatic example is the Islamic Republic of Iran, which has adopted the term "ideology" (spelled *idiolozhi* in Persian script, following the French pronunciation) as part of the definition of Islam. In this very modern formulation, religiosity is not valued in itself; it is acceptable only to the degree that it demands practical and political implementation and institutionalization in society.

The most notorious case of a Christian category being imposed upon Islam is that of fundamentalism. The term itself originated in California just after 1900, when a Protestant evangelical group published a leaflet titled *The Fundamentals*, containing a list of obligatory beliefs. Outsiders then used the term "fundamentalist" to describe Christian evangelical groups, such as those who opposed the teaching of Darwinian evolution in the Scopes trial of 1920 in Tennessee. After the spectacular outbreak of the Iranian revolution in 1978–79, journalists turned to the term to describe the ideology of Ayatollah Khomeini and others. Due to the tendency of the media to focus on these groups, the terms "fundamentalist" and "Muslim" became almost inseparable; many newspaper readers who are not familiar with Islam assumed that all Muslims were fundamentalists. The term is confusing, because one could also easily assume that fundamentals are a good thing in religion, yet somehow the term "fundamentalist" has always been a kind of insult. Scholars of religious studies who use the term try to do so descriptively, applying it to secondary male elites who oppose secular state power and attempt to affect social and political policies by authoritarian and highly selective reference to sacred scriptures.[13] As a protest against secular modernism, fundamentalism may be said to be a significant factor in all major religious traditions; according to the Fundamentalism Project at the University of Chicago, as much as 20 percent of the following of any major religion may be described as having a fundamentalist character.[14] It is still hotly debated whether the term "fundamentalist" is worth using; some prefer to use the word "Islamist" to describe the antimodernist ideology of reform in Muslim countries.

Whatever the terminology one uses, it remains the case that

Muslim reformist movements represent only one tendency in contemporary Islamic thought. Without trying to privilege one position over another, it is easy to point to other traditional Muslim schools of thought and forms of local practice that exist with a greater or lesser degree of formal structure in many different countries. Following the principles of the study of religion, we need to take account of all this diversity, rather than accepting one prescriptive view, if we want to have a reasonably complete picture of what it means to be Muslim today.

CHAPTER 3

THE SACRED SOURCES OF ISLAM

What are the origins of the Islamic faith? Before one asks this question, one has to acknowledge that there are multiple approaches to the subject, each of which dictates different possible answers. If one begins, as non-Muslims tend to do, by assuming that Islam is a new phenomenon, radically breaking from the religions of the past, then one begins with the life of the Prophet Muhammad (570–632 C.E.) and goes forward, looking for differences or even deviations. In this perspective, Islam starts as a newcomer, and differences from previous religions are staked out in a competitive and critical manner. If, on the other hand, one assumes that there are continuities between the Islamic religion and previous traditions, as many Muslims do, then similarities become the focus of interest. From that point of view, one can look back on Islam as a fulfillment and reflection upon a centuries-old tradition of prophecy, which stretches back through Jesus to Moses and Abraham. Both of these positions are debatable, since they rest on essentially theological assumptions; neither view in itself is comprehensive enough to serve both insiders and outsiders. Here I would like to give attention to both external scholarship and internal statements of faith in providing brief accounts of the sacred sources of Islam in the Prophet Muhammad, the Qur'an, and the complex known as Islamic law.

The Seal of the Prophets:
The Prophet Muhammad

The Protestant approach to religion, at its most elemental, assumes that all the essentials are laid down in the foundation of a
religion. From this perspective, only the scripture, and perhaps
the extrascriptural actions and pronouncements of the founder
of the religion, can be considered of crucial importance and divine inspiration. Everything that comes later has secondary importance and is perhaps questionable as an innovation and even
a deviation due to human weakness. Yet the history of religion
reveals a growth and development of thought and an ongoing
reflection on the original sources, none of which can be considered irrelevant or superfluous, except from a dogmatic point of
view (the rise of Protestant Christianity itself, well more than
1,000 years after the life of Jesus, is arguably an example of such
a development). Islam, likewise, cannot be limited to the
"golden age" of the time of the Prophet in Medina. The community of believers has continued to elaborate and meditate
upon the themes that emerged from his life and teachings. The
importance of the Prophet Muhammad for the Islamic tradition is incalculably greater than one might suppose from the
negative diatribes of European Christians, and I begin this account of the sacred sources of Islam with reflections on the
Prophet. While the Qur'an as divine revelation may be the most
important resource of the Islamic tradition, we would not have
it in its present form without the Prophet Muhammad, and
therefore I start with him. Nevertheless, the importance of
Muhammad is not limited to those sources that can be dated

with certainty to his own lifetime. He has served as an ongoing model for ethics, law, family life, politics, and spirituality in ways that were not anticipated 1,400 years ago. There are few people in history who have had a greater impact on humanity, and it is through the historical elaboration of tradition that we must seek to understand that impact.

Christian scholars engaged in the "quest for the historical Jesus" found it very difficult to separate a purely historical Jesus from the Jesus of faith. While at first glance it seems that the life of Muhammad is much more fully documented by contemporary sources, on closer examination one finds it is equally hard to isolate the historical Muhammad from the Muhammad of faith. This is not necessarily a problem. Most Christians do not expect to understand Jesus through an equivalent of the television news, with a popular anchorman reporting live on events at the Sea of Galilee. Nor do they think of Jesus in terms of a dry narration of facts from an encyclopedia. Instead, they are personally engaged with Jesus through scripture, which is treated as a living witness to divine truth, and by prayer and other practices tied to the holy days of the year. Art, architecture, music, literature, and film have all been used to convey imaginatively the religious importance of Jesus. Similarly, the significance of Muhammad for Muslims has been made plain not only by the Qur'an and other textual sources but also through stories, poetry, calligraphy, and other arts. Major events in the life of Muhammad are recalled in the special calendar of the Muslim year. Inevitably, the growth of these traditions has included local inflections that vary from one place to another, expressed in different languages and cultures. While it is impossible to catalog all of these different views of Muhammad, it is important to acknowledge that many perspectives exist. During the twenty-three years that Muhammad received prophetic revelations, he played multiple roles, and in subsequent generations different groups fixed on that aspect of the Prophet's life that most interested them. The portraits that they present are accordingly partial and one-sided. As the great Persian poet Rumi said, "Everyone became my friend from his own opinion, and failed to seek my secrets within me."[1]

At this point in most standard treatments of Islam, it is customary to present a brief narrative summarizing the life of the Prophet Muhammad from a historical point of view, providing a standard consensus based on what scholars have sifted from available materials.[2] Yet the earliest written sources address concerns very different from what modern historians seek. The classical documents in Arabic provide nothing like a modern psychological biography. Aside from the Qur'an and hadith (see below), we have access primarily to accounts of his battles in the style of ancient Arab epic, praise of the Prophet's excellence (in prose and verse), Qur'an commentaries that seek to explain verses by references to Muhammad's life, and stories that place Muhammad in relation to prophets of the past. In short, Muhammad is presented in terms of the cultural and religious imperatives of a religious tradition.

While it is desirable to provide some basic information, particularly since many American readers are unfamiliar with the story, it would not do justice to the many-faceted character of Muhammad to begin with a dry, factual summary. Should one summarize the life of Jesus Christ as the career of a Jewish carpenter of uncertain paternity who turned itinerant preacher of Judgment Day and was executed as a rebel by the Romans? What if one considered the Buddha as a troubled prince who abandoned his throne and family responsibilities to live as a beggar? What meaning exists in a brief account of their external lives? The religious significance of such figures would be buried by such an approach, with its deceptive claims of historical objectivity that leaves aside the beliefs and devotion of generations.

Instead, let us begin with a religious artifact: a calligraphic portrayal of the Prophet according to a traditional account of his physical appearance. This brief description, ordinarily in the version provided by Muhammad's cousin and son-in-law 'Ali, is simple and straightforward. "Muhammad was middle-sized, did not have lank or crisp hair, was not fat, had a white round face, wide black eyes, and long eyelashes. When he walked, he walked as though he went downhill. He had the 'seal of prophecy' between his shoulder blades. . . . His face shone like the moon on the night of the full moon."[3] For centuries Muslims in the Ottoman Turkish regions have expressed their devotion to the Prophet by making exquisite calligraphic copies of this text (known as the *hilya*, or "adornment") and hanging them in places of honor in their homes and workplaces.

In figure 3.1, from the calligraphy of contemporary Pakistani artist Rasheed Butt, the description of Muhammad is contained within the main circular disk that is the heart of the composition. The text in this case comes from a Bedouin woman named Umm Ma'bad, who met Muhammad when he was making his historic journey to Medina:

"I saw a man, pure and clean, with a handsome face and a fine figure. He was not marred by a skinny body, nor was he overly small in the head and neck. He was graceful and elegant, with intensely black eyes and thick eyelashes. There was a huskiness in his voice, and his neck was long. His beard was thick, and his eyebrows were finely arched and joined together. When silent, he was grave and dignified, and when he spoke, glory rose up and overcame him. He was from afar the most beautiful of men and the most glorious, and close up he was the sweetest and the loveliest. He was sweet of speech and articulate, but not petty or trifling. His speech was a string of cascading pearls, measured so that none despaired

FIGURE 3.1

Hilyat al-Nabi ("Ornament of the Prophet"),
calligraphic composition by Rasheed Butt
(Photo courtesy of The Ackland Art Museum;
reproduced with the permission of Rasheed Butt)

of its length, and no eye challenged him because of brevity. In company he is like a branch between two other branches, but he is the most flourishing of the three in appearance, and the loveliest in power. He has friends surrounding him, who listen to his words. If he commands, they obey implicitly, with eagerness and haste, without frown or complaint." May God bless him and grant him peace. God, pray for and grant peace to Muhammad, your servant, your Prophet, and your messenger, the illiterate Prophet, and to his family and companions, and grant him peace. Written with the grace of God Most High by Rasheed Butt, may God forgive him.[4]

Four smaller disks containing the names of Muhammad's principal successors remind the viewer of the role of tradition in transmitting his legacy. Above in large letters are the words, "In the name of God, the Merciful, the Compassionate," the phrase that begins nearly every section of the Qur'an. Highlighted below the text is the phrase in which God announces the universal role of Muhammad: "We only sent you as a mercy for creation" (Qur'an 21:107). The framing of this description by God's words proclaiming the cosmic role of the Prophet signals the unique spiritual position that Muhammad holds.

This remarkable example of contemporary Islamic art indicates one way in which the Muhammad of faith is approached by believers. As an artistic creation, it is a calligraphic icon that represents the physical person of the Prophet without crossing into a visual portrait. Many Muslims used this artifact as a devotional aid. According to a saying of Muhammad recorded in one of the standard collections, "For him who sees my *hilya* after my death, it is as if he had seen me myself, and he who sees it, longing for me, for him God will make Hellfire prohibited, and he will not be resurrected naked at Doomsday."[5] Although there are miniature paintings depicting Muhammad in some medieval manuscripts, those were usually produced privately for elite patrons rather than as public religious art such as one sees in Christian churches. Muslims have largely rejected the representation of human and animal forms in deliberately religious art. But calligraphy, ideally suited to transmitting the word of God in a beautiful physical form, was the religious art par excellence in Muslim cultures. In this way, it was possible to have a symbolic reminder of the presence of the Prophet Muhammad without creating any kind of "graven image" that would be unacceptable to Muslim sensitivities.

It would be more accurate, however, to say that this artistic concept represents only one of the Muhammads of faith. There are many Muslims today who will find this representation strange, partly because this regional artistic tradition is not well known outside southeastern Europe, Turkey, and the eastern Mediterranean. More importantly, this calligraphic evocation of the Prophet calls attention to him as the one who intercedes with God on behalf of humanity; this is the Muhammad of grace. In reformist circles, the notion that any human being, even the Prophet, can intercede on behalf of others is often vehemently rejected as a kind of idolatry and worship of human beings. For them, another figure commands their attention: the Muhammad of authority. For those who revere the Muhammad of grace, the historical details of his life and his legal pronouncements are of less interest than his beauty and his compassion for those in need. There is an immense literature on the physical appearance of the Prophet, stressing his remarkable beauty and in the process creating legends of his miraculous deeds. This Muhammad is celebrated around the world in festivals marking his birthday. Although this kind of devotional practice is certainly more than 1,000 years old, today's reformists consider it an unpleasant and heretical innovation that has no basis in sacred texts. Saudi legal authorities have issued decrees in recent years denouncing the celebration of the Prophet's birthday as forbidden and blameworthy.

The Muhammad of authority is not necessarily in conflict with the Muhammad of grace. The Qur'an (33:21) calls the Prophet "a beautiful model," and subsequent generations carefully sifted oral tradition to find sayings and actions of the Prophet that could serve as ethical guidance and legal precedents. The Qur'an alludes to the special status of Muhammad and his closeness to God in a number of places. "Whoever obeys the messenger obeys God" (4:80). His position as representative of God made any agreement with him equivalent to an agreement with God. "Those who swear allegiance to you swear allegiance to God" (48:10). Although in some places the Qur'an declines to make distinctions among the prophets, Muhammad is singled out as "the seal of the prophets" (33:40), the one whose imprint on history is as final as a wax seal on a letter. Over the centuries it was typical for legal scholars to combine study of prophetic sayings with deep reverence for the Prophet. The sayings of Muhammad, known as *hadith* (Arabic for "report, news"), constitute a kind of secondary scripture for Muslims, with an authority exceeded only by the Qur'an. Muhammad from this perspective acted primarily as the source of legislation and morality. Since the Qur'an contains relatively few specific legal injunctions, it was natural for Muslims to turn to the far more extensive collections of reports of his sayings and deeds for precedents.

In the subsequent elaboration of Islamic law, the hadith sayings formed the body of material from which one could extract the Prophet's ethical and religious model of exemplary behavior (*sunna*). This prophetic example was, after the Qur'an, the second most important of the four recognized sources of Islamic law (scholarly consensus and reasoning by analogy were supplementary to Qur'an and sunna). So important was the concept of sunna or prophetic example that it became the basis for the name of the largest sectarian division in Islam, known as Sunni insofar as it claims to emulate the model of Muhammad. Collectors of hadith sayings sifted thousands of such reports for authenticity, using primarily the moral character of the oral transmitters as a guide to their authority. In modern times, European scholars have raised critical questions about the authenticity of the major collections of hadith reports, which were used to establish the prophetic sunna. Because it is always extremely tempting to have a proof text to back up one's position in a legal argument, as one tenth-century scholar remarked, "pious men are never so ready to lie as in matters of hadith." For this reason, Orientalist scholars cast doubt upon any quotations from the Prophet that seemed to have a clear and specific legal consequence; such an obvious legal application, in their view, meant that these reports were obviously forged, especially since many of them addressed specific issues that only arose many years after the time of the Prophet. This harsh criticism of hadith has not failed to have an effect on contemporary Muslim thought as well. Considerable debate has taken place regarding the extent to which hadith sayings can be relied on as a source of religious guidance. This is one additional reason for the exclusive focus on the Qur'an and rejection of subsequent tradition among some modern Muslim intellectuals.

Early theologians, particularly those of the Shi'i school, regarded the existence of prophets as a necessary corollary to God's mercy (the distinctive doctrines that separate the Shi'i from the Sunni will be discussed later). These scholars reasoned that mercy is one of the divine attributes and that, therefore, God would not deny his mercy to creation. Given the weakness and imperfection of human nature, it is impossible for humanity to overcome ignorance and suffering without the aid of divine knowledge. And how else should that knowledge be communicated to humanity, except through one among them who is chosen by God to deliver that message? The prophets are therefore regarded as the best of humanity, whom God necessarily preserves from sin, since otherwise they could not function as genuine moral and religious leaders. Only through divine inspiration can the knowledge of God's unity be revealed to humanity. Through this reasoning, the Shi'is observed that the appearance of a profound religious leader like Muhammad in the benighted ignorance of pagan Arabia is a perfect example of the providence and mercy of God.[6] While Muhammad is regarded as the last such prophet to be sent by God, Shi'i scholars consider that the divine mercy continues to function after his death through the office of the charismatic leaders known as the Imams, who are physical descendants of the Prophet. The Shi'i perspective claims both the Muhammad of authority and the Muhammad of grace but systematizes both concepts through a rigorous theology.

Yet another approach to prophecy came from the philosophers, who undertook an elaborate and ingenious interpretation based on Plato's concept of the philosopher-king. The tenth-century philosopher al-Farabi brilliantly joined Aristotelian cosmology with Islamic theology, declaring that the intellects that move the heavenly spheres are identical with the angels of revelation. A prophet, like a philosopher, has attained to union with the Active Intellect (also known as the angel Gabriel), so they have essentially the same consciousness. The difference lies in the public role of the prophet, who has the duty of revealing the religious law as a moral code and symbolic structure for all who are incapable of philosophical reasoning. From this perspective, while the ultimate truth of revelation is identical with the conclusions of metaphysics, religion as the public implementation of philosophy performs the roles of politics and ethics. Using Qur'anic language, al-Farabi says that all of the prophets and philosophers are "a single soul" (Qur'an 31:28 etc.). Like Augustine, he regards the particular religion adopted by the philosopher-king as a matter of divine dispensation according to the time and place. The philosophical interpretation of prophecy in a sense subordinated religion to philosophy and devalued history, esteeming Muhammad not so much for his individual characteristics as for the cosmic function he fulfilled. While this perspective remained limited to small circles of philosophers, it nonetheless had an important impact, particularly on those philosophically minded rulers who aspired to be the successors to the role of the Prophet, as God's representative and Muhammad's successor (*khalifa*, or caliph) on earth. Here, too, we find both the Muhammad of authority and the Muhammad of grace, but refracted through the lens of philosophy.

The fifteenth-century Persian philosopher and prime minister Jalal al-Din Davani appreciated both the transcendental position of the Prophet, as a recipient of divine light, and the necessity for him to be a normal man. Here is how he balanced the two aspects of Muhammad's existence:

Since the revered Chief of the Messengers (upon whom be prayers and peace) was the source of the majestic and beautiful divine lights, and the revealer of the effects of divine greatness and unlimited glory, he inspired awe to a remarkable degree. [Muhammad's pagan opponent] Abu Sufyan, when he was still a non-Muslim, came near the Prophet to make a treaty. When he returned, he said, "By God! I have seen many kings and leaders, and none of them inspired this fear and awe in my heart." The Prophet Muhammad's grace and friendliness were also extraordinary. One day a woman came before the Prophet, wishing to present a request. Indeed, because of the sparks of holy lights from the windows of the holy soul of the revered Prophet, his light was reflected on the four walls of that purified house. As her obvious astonishment increased, when the Prophet became aware of this, he said, "Do not fear; I am the son of an Arab woman who used to eat dried meat." The intention of the Prophet was to pacify the fear and awe from the heart of that woman, so that she could make her request known. Showing pride to the proud and humility to the poor and oppressed is part of the ethics of generosity.[7]

For this philosopher, Muhammad provided a model for justice by treating everyone as he or she deserved, whether it meant appearing as a powerful leader or as a humble, ordinary person.

These are by no means the only conceptions of Muhammad that Muslims have articulated. Among the Muhammads of faith one should also include, for instance, the socialist Muhammad, embodying modern ideals of social liberation and justice. The history of Muslim views of Muhammad until fairly recently has been dominated by an emphasis on his cosmic role as the main intercessor for humanity. Mystical concepts of Muhammad portrayed him not only as an ethical guide but also as the pre-eternal light from which God created the world.[8] The main shift in the past century has been, in part, a response to the stridently negative depictions of the Prophet created by European authors, though it also reflects the growth of bourgeois scientific rationalism in Muslim countries. No longer is the Prophet a mystical presence or a semimythical figure wielding apocalyptic powers; now he is viewed as a social and political reformer who coolly dealt with corrupt pagan opponents as he set up a society that would stand as the model for human perfection on earth. Supernatural events and miracles are de-emphasized to such an extent that the ascension of Muhammad to the presence of God, the subject of countless stories and commentaries in premodern Muslim literatures, recedes in the twentieth century to become for many a psychological event that in no way confers extraordinary status on the Messenger of God.

Keeping in mind this insistence on the multiplicity of the "Muhammads of faith," it is useful to turn to tradition for a brief snapshot of Muhammad and the world he lived in. It is widely held that Muhammad was born around 570 C.E. in the Arabian city of Mecca, then a trading center on the edge of the two great empires of the day, Rome (centered in Byzantium) and Persia. While the date of his birth is not exactly certain, it reflects the beginning of his career as a prophet around 610, customarily thought to have begun when he was forty years old, the standard number of completeness in Near Eastern lore. Muhammad's father died before the child's birth, and his mother succumbed not long after, so as an orphan he was raised by relatives from the powerful Quraysh tribe, which dominated Mecca at the time. Although he experienced the nomadic lifestyle of the Bedouin Arabs, Muhammad's own life centered on the urban environment, not the desert. In his early life he was a trader by profession and worked for a widow named Khadija. Early accounts of his journeys to Syria include encounters with Christian monks who recognized him as a prophet. Though Khadija was fifteen years older, she proposed marriage to him when he was twenty-five. When Muhammad began to receive his revelations, amidst his self-doubt Khadija was the one who had complete trust in him, becoming in effect the first Muslim.

He was, by all accounts, a charismatic person known for his integrity. His nickname al-Amin, "the trustworthy," is illustrated by numerous reports that even in his youth he was sought out as an impartial arbitrator. Some have argued that he experienced a gradual spiritual development, with extended periods of meditation and retreat in a cave on Mount Hira, not far from Mecca. Others believe that his religious awakening was very sudden, the product of powerful experiences of revelation that came upon him unannounced. Although the religious environment of pre-Islamic Arabia is hard to reconstruct, the message that Muhammad began to articulate was something of a surprise. At its most basic, the contrast can be stated as the concept of one God as opposed to a polytheistic paganism. Monotheism itself was by no means unknown in Arabia; there were groups of Jews and occasional Christian monks in the peninsula, and certain Arabs (known as the Hanifs) were evidently religious seekers of some sophistication. Nevertheless, the public religious life of Mecca centered on the cube-shaped temple known as the Ka'ba, which contained 360 idols dedicated to various gods, goddesses, and the Arabian spirits known as the jinn. At the same time, there were apparently ancient traditions that associated the Ka'ba with Abraham and his son Ishmael, the ancestors of the Arabs. In a sense, Muhammad's mission was to restore the primordial religion of the Prophet Abraham in Arabia and to cast out the false idols of paganism. He also clearly aimed at the moral reform of society.

When Muhammad began to preach these ideas, he was accepted slowly. After his wife Khadija, the next to embrace his message were a boy (his cousin 'Ali) and a slave (Zayd). The more powerful members of society were not quick to listen to his insistence on moral responsibility, the overwhelming creative power of God, and the importance of caring for the poor, widows, and orphans. They also ridiculed the notion of the resurrection of the dead and the final judgment by God in the afterlife. Most significantly, Muhammad's emphasis on the one true God and his rejection of polytheism posed a threat to the local power structure. The annual trade fair and pilgrimage festival centered on the Meccan temple was a chief source of income for the Quraysh tribe, and the tribal leaders did not like what they saw as a threat to their livelihood. Muhammad's clan relatives mostly protected him from the wrath of his opponents, although he was subjected to humiliation and abuse. But the persecution of his followers was serious enough to cause a number of them to emigrate to Ethiopia, where the Christian king received them warmly. Meanwhile, Muhammad struggled with the harsh reception afforded him by his community. It was reportedly during this dark time that he experienced the ascension to Paradise and the divine presence.

Muhammad's ascension, only briefly alluded to in a couple of places in the Qur'an, has been the subject of considerable elaboration in hadith reports and later literature. It is generally understood that the Qur'an refers to the ascension of Muhammad in this short passage: "Praise be to him who brought his servant by night from the Sacred Mosque to the Farthest Mosque, whose vicinity we have blessed, that we might show him our signs" (17:1). In the most common interpretation of this verse, the Sacred Mosque is identified as the shrine of Mecca, while the Farthest Mosque is considered to be Jerusalem (and, indeed, the great mosque adjacent to the Dome of the Rock in Jerusalem is known as al-Masjid al-Aqsa, the "Farthest Mosque").

As the story goes, God miraculously transports Muhammad from Mecca to Jerusalem and from Jerusalem through the various heavens, where he meets all the great prophets of the past; in some accounts, considerable extra detail is provided about Muhammad's encounters with the angels and with God. At the highest heaven, where the Prophet Moses resides, the two talk briefly until it is time for Muhammad to enter the divine presence, an encounter only elliptically described in the Qur'an (53:13–18):

> And he saw him by another place,
> By the lotus of the farthest edge,
> Near which is the paradise of refuge,
> When the lotus was veiled by what veiled it,
> His eye did not waver, nor did he transgress;
> He had seen one of the greatest signs of his lord.

When Muhammad returns, Moses asks him what God said. In an exchange that has a certain folk humor about it, Muhammad indicates that God instructed him to order his community to perform fifty prayers a day. "Fifty prayers a day!" responds Moses; "I know these people—they will never perform what you ask." Noting this objection, Muhammad follows the advice of Moses and returns to the presence of God to ask for a reduction. Returning with this favor granted, he informs Moses that the daily prayer requirement will now be forty-five. Again, Moses is incredulous and advises Muhammad to seek a further reduction. This sequence continues until at last Muhammad returns with the announcement that his community must pray to God five times a day. When Moses once more tries to convince him to get this reduced, Muhammad refuses and says that he is ashamed to make this request of his Lord.

This story purports to explain how the requirement of five daily prayers arose for the Muslim community. Behind this narrative is concealed a deeper point. On another occasion the Prophet observed that "ritual prayer is the ascension of the believer," a saying that is inscribed on the wall of many mosques. The motions of bowing, kneeling, prostration, and standing that comprise this sequence of ritual prayer can be understood in part as a reenactment or evocation of the Prophet Muhammad's ascension to the presence of God. As indicated earlier, spiritual virtue had been defined as praying as though you see God face-to-face or, failing that, praying as though God sees you. In this way the extraordinary spiritual experience of the Prophet in his ascension serves as a model for what the ordinary believer should focus on in regular worship.

The subsequent career of the Prophet Muhammad was increasingly involved with his role as leader of the new community that emerged in acceptance of his message. Despite his rejection by Meccan society, Muhammad was sought out by the leaders of the town of Yathrib, subsequently known as Medina ("the city," short for "the city of the Prophet"). Medina was experiencing conflict between its different tribal groups, and in accordance with Arab custom, they sought a mediator to arbitrate the situation. Representatives from Medina met Muhammad in Mecca and invited him to take on this role, which he accepted. Muhammad's followers gradually departed from Mecca, and he finally slipped away unobtrusively with a single companion, much to the chagrin of his Meccan opponents, who would have preferred keeping him under their eye. Muhammad now became the leader of Medina. Although it has been described as a theocracy, which would put Muhammad into a position analogous to Samuel among the Israelites as God's representative, the political order of Medina under Muhammad's authority was more complex. As shown by the document known as the Constitution of Medina, Medina was a polity composed of Muhammad's religious followers plus Jews and pagans, all of whom nonetheless accepted his position of leadership, at least in theory. From the beginning, therefore, it is clear that religious pluralism was a principle accepted as the basis for a Muslim society. In this respect Muslim politics was a radical departure from the example of Christian Rome, which did not tolerate rival faiths except when certain rulers found it useful for the moment to protect a minority such as the Jews.

Although the new Muslim community had temporarily prayed in the direction of Jerusalem, acknowledging the Abrahamic origins of their faith, the ongoing revelation of the Qur'an soon altered that by recognizing Mecca as the orientation of prayer. European scholars have tended to view this change as a symptom of Muhammad's failure to convince the Arabian Jews of his mission as a prophet; according to this theory, in his disappointment Muhammad elevated Mecca to the status of rival to Jerusalem in a nationalistic response to his rejection by the Jews. This simplistic reading betrays a cynical approach in assuming that the new revelation (unlike Judaism and Christianity) was fabricated as a response to changing political conditions. Such a prejudicial attitude does not consider how Muhammad systematically sought to go beyond the official representations of Judaism and Christianity to their ultimate revelatory source. Nor does it explain why even to the pagan Arabs the Lord of Mecca was the high god simply known as "the God" (*allah*), even if the character of the deity was not clearly thought out.

One of the characteristic issues of the Medinan phase of the Prophet's life was how to face political and military conflict. This arose in particular with two groups: the pagan rulers of Mecca and the Jewish tribes of Medina who were unsatisfied with Muhammad's leadership. He successfully opposed the Meccans in a series of raids and battles, and eventually the Muslim forces, including various allied nomadic tribes, proved so superior that the Meccans were forced to yield. Charges of treason and collaboration with the Meccans led to the expulsion of two of the major Jewish tribes, while members of a third tribe suffered execution and captivity (the details and extent of this incident are disputed). This was, in any event, a political conflict, and there was never any requirement that Jews and Christians should have to convert to Islam (this recognition of the "peoples of the book" was later extended to other religions such as Zoroastrianism and Hinduism). For this reason, scholars are suspicious about the letters allegedly written by Muhammad to the emperors of Rome and Persia in which he demanded their submission and their conversion to Islam. These letters are a much better fit with the world-conquering ambitions of the Arab empire that arose at the end of the seventh century. The pagan Arab tribes were, however, required to abandon their polytheism for Islam when they accepted the authority of the

Prophet. In the end, Muhammad entered Mecca at the head of an imposing force without opposition, and he extended amnesty to his former opponents.

Throughout the time that Muhammad acted as Prophet and political leader, he was also a husband and father, a man who was attracted to women and was intensely devoted to his family and children. After the death of Khadija, Muhammad married a number of wives; although some of these were political arrangements to cement tribal alliances, he physically consummated marriages with nine women and fathered several children. While his family affairs had their share of difficulties, they were clearly a central part of his life. Muhammad remarked in a hadith, "Three things in your world have been made lovely to me: perfume, women, and prayer is the delight of my eyes." This remarkable statement unites sensory pleasure, the attraction of the sexes, and deep religious sentiment; all of life, physical and spiritual, forms a single continuum. It is important to note that Muhammad's life, though in many respects exemplary for Muslims, is also, in part, exceptional. The legal possibility of four wives for Muslim men (which is comparatively rare in those countries where it is still permitted) clearly differs from the larger number of marriages afforded to the Prophet. The Prophet's wives were exceptional, too; they were forbidden to remarry after his death, and unlike other women, they alone were specifically required by the Qur'an (33:32, 33:53) to conceal themselves from men behind a curtain in their household. The widespread adoption of the custom of veiling, in part on the basis of aristocratic Greek and Persian models, is a separate development.

Christians typically have seen Muhammad's marriages as a mark against him, in comparison with the life of celibacy led by Jesus. The early Christian emphasis on virginity and the monastic way of life perhaps made it inevitable that Christians would reject Muhammad's marriages. St. Paul, who advised that "it is

better to marry than to burn," can hardly be called an enthusias-
tic champion of marriage. Celibacy was, after all, much better
suited to the early Christian anticipation of the apocalypse,
when there was no need to prepare for future generations.
Monastic celibacy and vows of chastity are on the retreat,
however, in modern Europe and America. While the Catholic
Church still insists on priestly celibacy in imitation of Jesus,
Protestant and Orthodox Christian churches for centuries have
dispensed with this aspect of the life of Jesus, rejecting both celi-
bate priesthood and (for most Protestants) monasticism. In
today's society, despite calls for sexual abstinence before marriage, popular entertainment and advertising are saturated with
enticing images of sexual fulfillment. As with Christian criticism of Muhammad's military activities, shock expressed at his
multiple marriages masks a considerable gap between ideal
and reality in Euro-American societies. Neither pacifism nor
celibacy has played more than a minor role in our modern social or political history, and advocates for these ideals are typically regarded as crackpots today. Thus it is more than ironic
when Christians reject Muhammad on the grounds that he was
both an effective leader and a zealous and affectionate husband
and father.

At the end of his life (Muhammad died in 632 C.E.), the
Prophet was head of a major community, having created alliances with all of the tribes of the Arabian Peninsula, probably
the first time that had occurred. What is more significant is that
his prophetic experience provided the basis of fervent ritual
practice, ethical ideals, and social structures that are deeply
etched into human history. Yet the way in which those ideals
and practices would play out depended on many unforeseeable
local adaptations.

The Word of God: The Qur'an

I recall when, as a graduate student at Harvard, I first went to the Widener Library to do some research on the Qur'an. Much to my surprise, the card catalog listing for the Qur'an (under the older spelling, Koran) gave a cross-reference to Muhammad as the author of the text. In contrast, the Bible was listed without any author. This library listing created a subtle contrast; while the Bible may have been of divine origin, the Qur'an was viewed as the composition of a human being. A Muslim reader, regarding the Qur'an as the actual Word of God, would no doubt find this librarian's classification objectionable. This example indicates how complicated it may be to approach the Qur'an for the first time. The assumptions that one brings to this effort will have a great deal to do with the result. Readers who wish to probe the Qur'an more deeply will need to go beyond these preliminary remarks, since I will mainly address here the most common assumptions and misconceptions that surround this sacred text of Islam.

It is, in fact, difficult to read the Qur'an as if it were an ordinary book. Its composition is very different from that of the Hebrew Bible or the New Testament; regardless of one's view of revelation, both of these texts contain multiple documents of different types assembled over a period of time by different hands. The Hebrew Bible contains extensive narratives and histories, together with prophetic writings, poetry, and didactic literature. The New Testament has four gospels by different writers describing the life of Jesus, the pastoral letters of St. Paul and others, a history of the early Christian community in Acts of the

Apostles, plus the apocalyptic Book of Revelation. In the case of the Christian scriptures, their selection and inclusion in the Bible (and the rejection of other writings) was the work of church councils. In contrast, the Qur'an is widely accepted as the accumulated revelations of the twenty-three years of the Prophet Muhammad's career, and it therefore is much more homogeneous as a text, with no signs of multiple authorship. This does not make it easy to classify, however.

When one considers the organization of the Qur'an, it is first of all apparent that it is divided into 114 books or sections known as suras, each of which is composed of varying numbers of verses called *ayas* ("sign, miracle"). With the exception of the first sura, a short prayer known as "The Opening," the rest are arranged roughly in order of decreasing size, with sura 2 ("The Cow") being the longest. In standard editions of the Qur'an, one typically finds that the heading of each sura identifies it as belonging to either the Meccan or the Medinan period of the Prophet's life. This basic distinction is useful, since many of the earlier passages show particular features of the Prophet's first preaching in Mecca: the creative power of God, God's unity, the resurrection and the afterlife, and the experiences of revelation. In contrast, the verses revealed in Medina typically emphasize legislative and social issues, with reflection on the difficulties faced by earlier prophets such as Moses. Within many suras, it is not unusual to find abrupt changes of subject, such as a sudden shift from a description of Paradise to the details of inheritance law.

As a result of this complex structure, the Qur'an contains very few extended narrative passages; the one major exception is sura 12, which contains the story of Joseph, which is emphatically introduced as "the most beautiful of stories." Yet the many allusions and references to stories of prophets such as Abraham, Moses, and Jesus presuppose that the audience is already familiar with the basic outlines of those narratives. In this sense, some Qur'anic passages are similar to poetic cycles that dwell on certain famous incidents to explain their importance but do not need to spell out every detail of the story.

Because of the challenging character of the Qur'anic text, many authorities from early times have suggested that those approaching it for the first time should not simply start reading the Qur'an from page 1. Instead, they should begin with the short suras at the end of the Qur'an. These are largely from the early Meccan period, and with their vivid depictions of the afterlife, God's creative power in nature, and the power of the prophetic experience, they form an excellent entry for understanding how the Qur'an works. It is also helpful if one can get some idea of the aesthetic experience of hearing the Qur'an, either through recordings or on websites.[9] Many non-Muslims have acknowledged that the Arabic verses of the Qur'an do indeed have a powerful aesthetic effect. The name "Qur'an" itself means recitation, and it assumes that the text is read aloud rather than silently. The oral component of the Qur'an is a major part of its transmission and reception. When modern authorities in Egypt decided to print the Qur'an early in the twentieth century, this shift from handwritten manuscript to a new technology raised many questions. What is most remarkable about this process is that the new printed edition of the Qur'an was certified by oral transmitters who were viewed as authoritative custodians of the sacred text.

Readers familiar with debates over the historical composition of the Bible may wonder how the Qur'an originated. Biblical scholars have argued against Moses as author of the first books of the Bible, seeing instead a series of editors who refashioned narratives, legal codes, poetry, and prophecy over a period of many centuries. Likewise, the Gospels of the New Testament are believed to have been written down roughly between 90 and 150 C.E. When was the text of the Qur'an finalized? This question is complicated by the traditional belief that the Prophet Muhammad was illiterate, a view that reinforces the doctrine of the miraculous character of the Qur'an; if the Prophet could neither read or write, so the argument goes, then his reception of a text of surpassing beauty and wisdom must be a divine revelation. The Arabic term that is often translated as "illiterate" (*ummi*) has another plausible interpretation: it could mean, instead, that Muhammad is the "Gentile" prophet sent to the nation (*umma*) of the Arabs. Symbolically, the illiteracy of the Prophet is parallel to the doctrine of the virgin birth of Jesus, as many commentators have observed. In either case, the Word of God (whether in the form of the Qur'an or the son of God) comes into existence through divine agency rather than human initiative. Whether the Prophet was illiterate or not is debatable, especially since he was a merchant by profession and is said to have traveled widely. The revelations that he delivered seem to have been written down, in part, during his lifetime, although the accounts that we have also take for granted an amazing capacity for oral memorization among the Arabs.

According to the standard account, Muhammad's successors became concerned over the preservation of the Qur'an after several notable memorizers of the text died in battle. Verses that had been preserved written on branches, on stone, and on the hearts of men are said to have been copied out on sheets. Nevertheless, it eventually became apparent that different copies of the Qur'an contained noticeable variations. This caused 'Uthman, the third caliph (who ruled 644–52 c.e.), to establish an authoritative version of the text, and he ordered the destruction of all other copies. Interestingly, one highly respected Qur'anic scholar, Ibn Mas'ud, refused to surrender his Qur'an. Commentaries and other scholarly writings, in fact, preserve many minor variations on the received Qur'anic text. How significant are these variations?

If one looks to the history of biblical texts in comparison, it is significant that among the 5,000 surviving manuscripts of the Greek New Testament, no two are identical. For the most part, the differences are insignificant verbal variations that are easily understood as by-products of the scribal process of copying. Occasionally, however, there are manuscripts in which copyists have made deliberate changes to important words that had implications for religious debates within the early Christian Church.[10] The Qur'anic text has a certain amount of variation, which has even been codified into seven major schools of recitation and seven minor variations on those. The differences among these recitations of the Qur'an consist mainly of trivial alternatives in spelling and pronunciation of particular words, though there are occasional significant differences.[11] Although there were some early sectarian groups, particularly among the Shi'is, who alleged that certain important revelations had been suppressed, it is almost impossible to find any serious arguments in favor of this thesis today. A few modern European scholars have proposed revisionist accounts of the collection and history of the Qur'an, ranging from alternative dating of different sections to a hypercritical thesis that suggests that the Qur'an was composed a couple of centuries after the death of the Prophet. Most of this discussion was safely buried in obscure academic journals, but the Qur'an unexpectedly became a burning issue toward the end of the twentieth century.

The 1989 publication of Salman Rushdie's novel *The Satanic Verses* turned the question of the Qur'an as revelation into an international controversy. Rushdie, a British-based novelist born into an Indian Muslim family, had distinguished himself with a series of bitingly sardonic works of fiction, including *Shame* (a satire on politics in Pakistan) and *Midnight's Children* (a "magical realism" interpretation of the 1947 partition of India and Pakistan). Rushdie had been educated in England, and while he had received widespread applause and recognition there, *The Satanic Verses* was in part aimed at depicting the agonies and alienation of postcolonial Asian immigrants in England. In the midst of this complicated book occurs an extended dream sequence offering a strange account of a Middle Eastern prophet, obviously based on the Prophet Muhammad. A narrator named Salman, who acts as a scribe in recording the prophet's revelations, inserts his own words into the transcript as a kind of test, and much to his surprise, the prophet accepts them as part of the revelation. In his responses to later criticism, Rushdie tried to present this dream sequence as a postmodern depiction of the struggle of the artist or poet against religious authoritarianism, but it was widely perceived as an attack on the credibility of the Qur'an as an authentic divine revelation to Muhammad. His disclaimers were not helped by the novel's account of prostitutes in a brothel who were obviously modeled on the wives of Muhammad. In part thanks to an aggressive advertising campaign by the publisher, the novel aroused an immense outcry among Muslims around the world. The peak of the protest came on Valentine's Day in 1989, when Iran's supreme leader, Ayatollah Khomeini, delivered a legal opinion (*fatwa*) stating that Rushdie's novel was blasphemy and the author deserved a death sentence. It is worth noting that *The Satanic Verses* also includes a satirical section apparently aimed at Khomeini himself; he appears as a mullah who is so severe that even pictures on walls run away at his approach.

What did this controversy really have to do with the Qur'an? Leaving aside the complex questions of artistic freedom and hate speech raised by the case, it is clear that Rushdie was inspired by the issue of the so-called Satanic verses. This is the name that European scholars gave to a report suggesting that the Prophet Muhammad inadvertently accepted a suggestion from the devil, thinking it was a divine revelation. Amazingly,

the verses would have permitted the Muslims to continue wor-
shiping the pagan goddesses of the Arabs alongside the one true
God (Muslim scholars refer to this report as "the lofty cranes,"
citing the words allegedly used in these verses to describe the
goddesses as high-flying birds). A subsequent revelation is then
said to have rejected or abrogated this insinuation, however.
Most scholars now consider this report, which only occurs in
two early compilations, to be dubious, for several reasons: it has
weak transmitters, it is a suspiciously neat fit with the doctrine
of Qur'anic abrogation (whereby a later revelation may invali-
date an earlier one), and the story also has anachronistic details
that make it questionable. It would have been inserted, moreover, in an extremely unlikely place, directly following the description of Muhammad's ascension to the divine presence
(Qur'an 53:1–18). Implausible though this incident may be, it
is, like many thousands of other dubious reports about the
Prophet, transmitted in hadith collections; some of these reports were undoubtedly invented later to prove various points.
Muslim scholars preserved all this material as part of an archival
collection, even when they explicitly recognized it as problematic. What is striking is that early European Orientalists believed
that this isolated report was undoubtedly true, precisely because
they thought that it conclusively demonstrated something they
already took for granted: the falsity of Muhammad's revelation.
Rushdie had, in effect, internalized the Orientalist attack on the
Prophet Muhammad. It was this voluntary alienation from Islamic identity, more than anything else, that motivated the outrage that Muslims expressed against Rushdie's novel.

When European and American media have turned their attention to the question of Qur'anic revelation, they have continued to do so with the breathless expectation that new discoveries would turn traditional Muslim attitudes upside down. Such
was the case with a 1999 *Atlantic Monthly* article titled "What Is

the Koran?"[12] Citing the discovery of manuscripts in Yemen containing variations on the text of the Qur'an, this article strongly hinted that Muslim belief in the Qur'an as the Word of God would be seriously undermined by historical criticism. It is true that there is a genuine scholarly debate focusing on the lack of clearly dated Arabic manuscripts of the Qur'an prior to about 700 C.E. (the earliest dated Qur'anic text is the inscriptions in the Dome of the Rock in Jerusalem, from 692 C.E.). One group of scholars, following the work of John Wansborough, actually argues that the text of the Qur'an was not finalized for at least 200 years after the death of the Prophet. This argument, oddly enough, rests on speculative analogies rather than alternate documentary proof, so it is impossible either to prove or to disprove. The Yemeni manuscripts mentioned by the *Atlantic Monthly* article do not appear to have any startling or major changes but belong to the class of minor textual variations that have been known for centuries. There are other European scholars who maintain that the text of the Qur'an as we have it goes back to the very early years of the Muslim community. Much depends on the presuppositions with which this issue is approached.

The most peculiar thing about recent media treatments of the Qur'an is the tendency to privilege the modern reformist or fundamentalist interpretation as the only true representative of Islamic thought. Certainly one of the notable tendencies of modern history worldwide has been the fundamentalist insistence on so-called literal interpretation, which is used as a platform for resistance against secularism in the public sphere. This kind of modern globalizing fundamentalism has been especially prominent in American Christianity, and it may also be found in other religions, including Islam. Yet in making comparisons, Europeans and Americans generally assume that liberal and tolerant interpretations of scripture are typical of Judaism and Christianity, while for some reason Islam alone is exclusively dominated by violent fundamentalism. They further assume that religious tolerance is somehow intrinsic to Christianity (and by extension Judaism), rather than being a result of disgust with the religious wars of European Catholics and Protestants.

A recent cover article for *Newsweek* magazine, "In the Beginning, There Were the Holy Books," wonders if Islam is inherently intolerant and argues that in the Qur'an, "aggressive verses have fired Muslim zealots in every age."[13] Strangely, the one Qur'anic verse that is cited (9:14) refers in context to battles with Arab pagans, and the article does not provide a single example of any later Muslim reading this text and deciding that it is imperative to kill Christians or Jews; such a conclusion would actually be contrary to historical principles of Islamic law that guarantee the rights of Christians and Jews. This article further maintains that Israeli commandos and Christian Crusaders have killed without being under the inspiration of scripture or messianic example. The Qur'an, we are told, is believed to be "God's eternal word," unlike the Bible—an assertion that would be challenged by a significant number of Jewish rabbis and Christian ministers. These dubious examples of not-so-religious violence do not explain why Muslims are supposed to be motivated exclusively by religion, while Jews and Christians evidently have more complicated lives. While it is true that Osama bin Ladin, a man who was trained as an engineer, has interpreted the Qur'an (including the verse cited above) in order to justify horrible violence, he himself refers in detail to twentieth-century history as the situation he wishes to remedy; his violence, in other words, is political and has political roots in recent history. His self-taught interpretation of the Qur'an, moreover, systematically takes verses out of context and ignores contrary views in traditional religious scholarship, grimly seeking to impose a predetermined conclusion in favor of unlimited warfare against non-Muslims.[14] In this respect, he is no different from any Christian or Jewish extremist who proclaims himself against the world (like David Koresh) as the only righteous interpreter of God's word. Strangely, media outlets like *Newsweek* regard fundamentalists as the only true Muslims, and so they replicate and reinforce the very fundamentalist mentality that so appalls them.

One of the main misunderstandings of the Qur'an relates to the primacy of the original Arabic text. This stands in contrast to the Christian Bible, since the Greek New Testament was already a translation of what Jesus and his disciples discussed in Aramaic. Subsequent versions of the Bible followed in Latin and, after the Reformation, in the main European languages. Modern missionary societies have produced literally hundreds of translations of the Bible into every conceivable tongue. Like Orthodox Jews with Hebrew and Indian Brahmins with Sanskrit, Muslims continue to use the original language of their revelation, particularly in the daily performance of prayers. Arabic thus becomes a sacred language in this religious practice, despite the fact that it is not the native language of the vast majority of Muslims; since only about 18 percent of Muslims are Arabs, non-Arabs chant it as a foreign language, much as Catholics did with the Latin mass prior to the Vatican II reforms of the 1960s. The prestige of the Qur'an in Arabic is therefore immense, and it is regarded as an inimitable miracle; translation of the Qur'an, in the strictest sense, is therefore impossible. This opinion did not prevent certain early authorities from permitting non-Arabs to recite Qur'anic prayers in Persian translation, and for at least 1,000 years there have been interlinear translations of the Qur'an and commentaries written in other languages. It is very common today to see copies of the Qur'an with the translation into the local language alongside the Arabic. Nevertheless, a number of otherwise well-informed Europeans and Americans are under the impression that interpretation of the sacred text is not possible for Muslims, since their engagement with the original text enforces a literal acceptance of it.

This misconception illustrates once again the tendency to assume that all Muslims are fundamentalists. In reality, many different traditions of interpretation of the Qur'an are to be found in the history of Islam. One of the earliest commentaries, that of Muqatil ibn Sulayman (d. 767), emphasizes the need to understand multiple meanings of words, each of which can have several different aspects. Some commentaries, like that of Tabari, are vast compilations of sometimes conflicting oral reports, transmitted as hadith from the first generations of Muslims. There are commentaries that systematically argue a sectarian interpretation, as seen in the many productions of Shi'i writers; a prominent modern representative of this school is the leading Iranian scholar 'Allama Tabataba'i. Mystical interpretation was the hallmark of the Sufis, who compiled many works reflecting their meditations about the internal sense of the Qur'an.[15] Philosophers and theologians who had drawn deeply on the writings of Aristotle and Plato applied these insights to the understanding of the sacred text as well. The existence of these many traditions of commentary underlies an important point: the average Muslim in premodern times (like the average Christian or Hindu) was not literate and necessarily relied upon the authoritative knowledge of religious experts, which was accumulated over centuries of tradition. This means that in premodern Muslim societies we do not find the Protestant model of scriptural interpretation—the believer alone with the sacred text, without the mediation of tradition. Instead, it was necessary for the average believer to turn to qualified authorities. Experts did not attempt to read the text in an individualistic fashion but relied on the many-layered discoveries of their predecessors. Far from being a faith that avoids interpretation of scripture, Islam has been based on a rich and complex heritage with multiple ways of thinking about the Qur'an.

Another point that needs clarification is the role of the Qur'an as a source for Islamic law. There is no doubt that the prescriptions and prohibitions of the Qur'an have an enormous prestige, and in cases where they could be clearly applied, they have had a dominant authority. Nevertheless, of 6,346 verses in the Qur'an, only about 500—less than one-tenth of the total— have the form of law. The bulk of the sacred text thus consists of pieces of narrative, depictions of the afterlife and the power of God, and injunctions to have faith in God. Among the verses that have the force of legal prescription or prohibition, a great many are concerned with prayer and the religious duties of alms, fasting, and pilgrimage. Subjects such as inheritance, marriage, and divorce are indeed addressed in several passages, and there is a very small number of verses on what we would call criminal law. The Qur'an is therefore very far from being a complete code of laws that could serve as the basis for a state, whether in premodern times or today. While early legal scholars gave priority to the Qur'an as a source of law, it was unavoidable to supplement it with the example of the Prophet as revealed in hadith, with the consensus of scholars, and with the individual opinions of jurists based on analogy; all of this together formed the complex of Islamic law as an ideal, usually known as *shari'a*. In practice, premodern Islamic law was inevitably accompanied by extensive systems of administrative law created by imperial bureaucracies as well as by pre-Islamic custom and tribal law. In many cases, administrative law and local custom superseded Islamic law. With the arrival of European colonial powers in many Muslim countries in the nineteenth century, the rulers dismantled existing legal systems and imposed European legal codes wholesale, usually retaining only aspects of Islamic law relating to the personal and private sphere of marriage, divorce, and inheritance. Postcolonial Muslim countries have engaged in varying degrees of Islamizing experimentation with their legal systems, but in all these cases, modern legislators, bureaucrats, and ideologues (mostly without traditional legal training) are defining Islamic law in the name of the nation-state. This is a far cry from the highly developed tradition of Islamic legal scholarship that was intertwined with medieval empires. So when we speak of Muslim societies, this does not mean societies that are governed exclusively by Islamic law, since such societies did not exist; it is much less possible, therefore, to imagine societies ruled entirely by the Qur'an.

Although non-Muslims in recent years have imagined the Qur'an primarily as the ideological source for political activism, if we reconsider it as a religious text, its true importance becomes clear. Even, or especially, for those who do not know Arabic, the Qur'an is on their tongues and in their hearts as a direct sign of God's activity in the world. In a very real sense, the Qur'an as the Word of God for Muslims is parallel to Jesus as the Word of God for Christians. If one extends this analogy into religious practice, the most important ritual for Christians is Holy Communion or the Eucharist, by which the believer assimilates the body and blood of Jesus either in reality (for Catholics) or symbolically (for Protestants). In a similar way, when a Muslim recites the Qur'an, the Word of God is expressed directly on the tongue in a way that is charged with divine power. It is this experience that makes the Qur'an such a central part of Muslim religious life.

CHAPTER 4

ETHICS AND LIFE IN THE WORLD

Islamic Religious Ethics

It is customary in books that survey the Islamic faith to present a summary and overview of basic religious practices and beliefs. The problem with the textbook approach is that it outlines these catechisms and religious requirements in the abstract, without much reference either to multiple schools of thought or to the history of Islamic religious practice in different regions. In this respect, it can be difficult to distinguish between a textbook summary of basic practices and the preaching or religious instruction that one might encounter in a mosque (the equivalent of a Sunday school version of Christianity). This is even true with what are usually called the five pillars of Islam (that is, profession of faith, ritual prayer, fasting during the month of Ramadan, giving alms, and performing pilgrimage to Mecca). While there is nothing wrong with that approach in prescriptive teaching for the faith community, it is the aim of this book to offer a descriptive interpretation of the range of Islamic history and practice.

Though it is certainly true that there are commonalities of faith and practice that are shared widely by many Muslims, a historical and nonsectarian approach has to take account of differences as well. It is equally true that certain Muslim religious authorities lean heavily on the concept of Islamic unity. While the unity of the ideal religious community is certainly an important symbol, it is not a fact, nor has it ever been. Some Muslims have responded defensively to historical accounts of conflicting notions of Islamic belief and practice, charging that foreign Orientalists are stirring up trouble by dividing Muslims against one another. This notion of Western conspiracy, which may sound good rhetorically, is simply not true.

Substantial differences of belief and practice, for instance, characterize the Sunni majority versus the Shi'i (or Shi'ite) minority, although in theory all agree about the important practices mentioned above. The differences between Shi'i and Sunni range from how one places the hands during ritual prayer to whether temporary marriage is allowed, and they include major disagreements about the succession to Muhammad's authority and the nature of God's attributes. An interesting example is the Shi'i practice of performing the prostrations of ritual prayer by placing the forehead on a clay pillow taken from the earth of Kerbela, the pilgrimage city in Iraq that is the site of the martyrdom of the Prophet's grandson, Imam Husayn (Husayn died in 680 C.E. while leading a small military force in rebellion against a tyrannical caliph). Shi'is justify the use of this clay pillow on the grounds of both purity and reverence, although Sunnis do not employ it and regard it as completely irrelevant.[1] Rather than attempting to provide a catalog of Islamic beliefs and practices in all their bewildering detail, I propose here to look at examples that can shed light on how Islamic religious tradition plays out in the contemporary world. The discussion that follows concentrates on illuminating the examples at hand rather than striving for comprehensiveness.

When we turn to the subject of Islamic ethics, that is, the ideal norms of behavior that a Muslim community strives for, we need to take stock of a complex situation. The standard Arabic word for ethics, *akhlaq*, is actually a good parallel to both the Greek notion of ethics and the Roman concept of mores (from which we derive the term "morality"). In all three cases, we are dealing with a plural noun having to do with customs and correct modes of behavior. When we engage in systematic reflection on these modes of behavior, philosophical ethics becomes the science or theory of how one should act. Ethics become religious when the ideal norms of behavior derive from divine authority or important religious figures. To put the contrast sharply, we can know that certain things are right or wrong on the basis of our own reasoning (philosophical ethics), or we may know that they are right or wrong simply because God tells us so (religious ethics). In practice, most ethical systems combine both reasoning and authority to come to their conclusions about correct action. Islamic religious ethics rarely took on an entirely authoritarian aspect, since legal theorists consistently sought to find intentions and purposes in sacred texts. This kind of ethical reasoning was necessary to deal with the new situations not addressed in scripture that inevitably arose. In addition, while ethics in largely Muslim societies certainly derives in part from religious sources such as the Qur'an, hadith, and Islamic law, there is a great deal of normative behavior that comes from local custom or from major pre-Islamic cultures, including the heritage of Greek philosophy. While some features of local custom (like the celebrated hospitality of the pre-Islamic Arabs) are widely imprinted on different Muslim cultures, there are many features of local normative behavior that are limited to very specific contexts, such as matrilineal inheritance in the Maldive islands or the pilgrimage rituals at saints' shrines in the Moroccan mountains.

The Qur'an is the most highly revered source of the norms of correct behavior, since it is regarded as the word of God. The foundation for ethical obligation in the Qur'an is traced to the covenant established between God and humanity at the beginning of creation (Qur'an 7:172): "When your lord brought out their offspring from the children of Adam, from their backs, and made them testify to themselves: 'Am I not your lord?' They said, 'Yes, we have borne witness.'" It was in this pre-eternal moment that the destinies of all humanity were sealed, and the standard commentators view this as a statement of divine predestination. Those who answered "yes" would be the obedient servants of God, and those who did not reply would be rebels. This primordial scene becomes the charter both for ethics, as an acknowledgment of divine authority, and for spirituality, as a testimony to the intimate relationship between God and humanity.

It has been pointed out previously that the Qur'an contains relatively few clear prescriptions that could be construed as legal ordinances, although it has frequent and abundant verses urging the believers to reflect upon the power of God as manifest in creation and in the human soul. Divine authority is not merely asserted but is presented as a conclusion that should be clear to anyone with an open mind. "We shall show them our signs on the horizons and in themselves, until it is clear to them that 'he is the truth'" (41:53). Gratitude for God's favors and blessings is the appropriate human response, so that obedience to divine command follows naturally. Ingratitude and rejection of God (both implied by the Arabic word *kufr*) are intellectual errors as well as displays of arrogance. So even if the Qur'an does not provide guidance for every conceivable detail, it points to the development of a moral consciousness and human responsibility to God—to pray as if you see God, and if you do not, to know that God sees you. The subsequent working out of Islamic ethical thought begins from this point, although a number of additional authoritative texts come into play besides the Qur'an.

A good example of how Islamic texts function as sources of correct behavior would be one of the standard compilations of the hadith reports of the sayings and actions of the Prophet Muhammad. There are many such collections, but one of the most useful is the *Niche for Lamps* of al-Khatib al-Tabrizi (d. 1337), which is still a standard resource at major Islamic academies such as Deoband in India. It is interesting to see the extensive list of chapter topics that are covered in this subject-oriented collection.

1. Faith
2. Religious Knowledge
3. Purity
4. Ritual Prayer
5. Funerals
6. Alms
7. Fasting
8. Virtues of the Qur'an
9. Invocations
10. The Names of God
11. Pilgrimage
12. Commerce
13. Marriage
14. Freed Slaves
15. Punishments
16. Governing and Justice
17. Struggle (Jihad)
18. Hunting and Sacrifice
19. Foods
20. Clothing
21. Medicine and Divination
22. Dreams
23. Manners
24. Softening the Heart
25. Rebellion

These major divisions are then followed by sections on the events taking place at the resurrection, with additional biographical materials on the qualities of the Prophet Muhammad and his followers. It is challenging to come up with a concept that unites all the topics covered in this collection. Nearly the first half is taken up with topics that are clearly religious, but the rest covers the affairs of politics, economics, family, and other aspects of ordinary life.

As an authoritative text, the *Niche for Lamps* presents the statements and actions of the Prophet Muhammad as transmitted by a series of recognized intermediaries. In a scholarly fashion the text presents explanations of difficult words and commentaries on thorny subjects in notes on the margins. It is clear that the sayings and deeds of Muhammad are meant to serve as the models that should be imitated by the faithful. It was the work of hadith scholars to collect and arrange the sayings on the basis of trustworthy transmission. Another group of scholars specializing in law would then use these sayings as part of the materials on which they based general legal principles. Specialists in jurisprudence could apply these principles to theoretical cases that had not been dealt with in the Qur'an or hadith, and acting judges could deliver decisions in cases brought to courts of law. It is important to recall that hadith was only one of the sources of Islamic law, alongside the Qur'an, consensus of scholars, and analogical reasoning. Islamic legal specialists went further and investigated the purposes or intentions that they considered to be implicit in the law. These were the preservation of religion, life, offspring, property, and rationality.[2] In addition, Islamic law itself was only one part of premodern Muslim societies, since the application of law took place through separate administrative courts, royal decree, and tribal custom, in addition to courts specializing in Islamic law.

The technical details of the evolution of Islamic law and its complex application in different regions are beyond the scope of this work, but it is tempting to regard the complex of materials in the hadith collection as illustrating a concept of religious ethics that is quite broad. It is religious because the authoritative value of the examples cited derives in principle from the religious authority of the Prophet, rather than from independent reasoning as such (although interpretation inevitably comes into play). It is extensive because it includes religious ritual as well as ethical behavior in society. It is especially interesting to see the range of subjects covered in the chapters on "Manners" and "Softening the Heart." The first of these is a comprehensive term that covers items such as greetings, asking permission, shaking hands, standing and sitting, laughing, poetry, silence, promises, kindness, love of God, modesty, anger, pride, and injustice. The second is an even more psychological category, designed to elicit sympathy for others, and includes sections on poverty, hope, patience, hypocrisy, weeping, fear, and advice. Naturally, the examples given in all these topics represent ideal forms of behavior rather than what is actually encountered in any given situation, but that is the nature of ethics.

A few examples of hadith from this collection, in which members of the early Muslim community narrate sayings of Muhammad, will illustrate the materials that could be used as a basis for Islamic religious ethics. Some of these sayings make it clear that a great deal of responsibility for ethical behavior lies with the individual believer.

> Ibn 'Umar said, "The Messenger of God (God bless him and grant him peace) said, 'Obedience to authority is incumbent on the Muslim man regarding what is desirable and undesirable, as long as he is not commanded to sin; but if he is commanded to sin, there should be no obedience.'"
>
> Al-Miqdad ibn Ma'd Yakrib said, "The Messenger of God (God bless him and grant him peace) said, 'No one eats better food than what he has made himself.'"
>
> 'Abd Allah ibn 'Umar said, "A man came to the Messenger of God (May God bless him and grant him peace), and asked permission to engage in righteous struggle (jihad). He re-

plied, 'Are your parents living?' The man said, 'Yes.' He replied, 'So struggle on their behalf.' This is a confirmed hadith. But in another transmission, it reads: 'So return to your parents and take good care of them.' "

While it is not possible to summarize here the many thousands of similar hadith reports, one can see how wide a range of topics could be covered by a religious ethics based on the prophetic example.[3]

As in the Jewish tradition, Islamic religious ethics imperceptibly merges with religious law. In this sense, both Jewish and Islamic traditions stand in contrast with the Christian emphasis on freedom from the law, as spelled out by St. Paul in the New Testament. Because of the overwhelming importance of grace in Christian theology, the development of legal codes was initially left to secular authorities, mainly the Roman Empire. When the Church at length developed its own internal legal mechanisms in the form of canon law, the ecclesiastical system ended up also taking the Roman legal codes as its basis. Because of the typically minority status of Jews in premodern times, Jewish law was usually limited in application to Jewish religious practices and internal community affairs. But the complex of Islamic law as an ideal, the *shari'a*, addressed politics, economics, and family, in addition to religious practice and ethical behavior, and it was an important source for Muslim societies. What is distinctive, then, about Islamic law is that it had a significant historical role in the development of major empires in the Mediterranean region and in Asia, although it was far from being the only or even the dominant element in those societies.

To what extent does Islamic religious ethics differ from other ethical systems? There is a fair amount of overlap between the ethical prescriptions of Islamic law and many commonly acknowledged ethical injunctions from other religious traditions, such as prohibitions on murder, theft, adultery, lying, and other crimes. At the same time, there are distinctive rules, particularly in the area of ritual, that distinguish Muslims from other communities; the rules for purity in relation to ritual prayer, for example, are very specific to Islamic practice. Some distinctive customs have their analogies in Judaism, such as dietary prohibitions on foods such as pork and the requirement that animals be sacrificed in the name of God before they can be lawfully eaten. What sets apart Islamic ethics from other systems is its historical basis in Arabian society and in the prophetic experience of Muhammad; all this was interpreted and molded by subsequent generations in the light of multiple cultural contexts, ranging from Africa to southeastern Europe, China, and Indonesia. Some Muslim scholars insisted on emphasizing customary practices that set Muslims apart from other communities even in matters of dress, and they resolutely forbade Muslims from participating in non-Muslim festivals such as Easter. In their view, any innovation beyond the norms of Muslim society at the time of the Prophet was reprehensible. At the same time, new observances arose, such as the commemorations of the Prophet's birthday and his ascension to heaven, or the lamentations for the Shi'i martyrs. There was frequently overlap in local religious customs with other religious communities such as Christians and Hindus.

Distinctive Muslim legal and ethical norms were justified by both authority and reason. As an example, one may consider the Islamic injunction against drinking alcohol and other intoxicants, which stands apart from most Christian and Jewish positions. To the extent that such ethical and legal norms derive their authority from God, they may not require the support of reasoning or practical benefits. There is no obvious reason why pork is forbidden in both Jewish and Islamic law, although one can argue that the pig is a habitually unclean animal (the modern notion that pork was prohibited as a health measure prior to the invention of refrigeration is unconvincing). The Qur'an simply prohibits the consumption of already dead animals, blood, pork, and flesh that has been sacrificed to a pagan deity, without clarifying the different reasons for each of these prohibitions; determining the purposes of such prohibitions was left to later jurists. Thus Muslim jurists maintained that the prohibition of alcohol and intoxicants has as its purpose the preservation of one's intellect. The development of Islamic law as a system was therefore a combination of revelation and reason.

Since Islamic ethics includes social and political issues, it covers questions of war and peace as well. Many are familiar with the term "jihad" as meaning "holy war," although that translation is really the application of Christian terminology. "Jihad" means properly "struggle," in the sense of struggle or effort for truth. A related term is *ijtihad*, which is the effort of independent legal reasoning and interpretation by a fully qualified jurist. Jihad was certainly applied to military struggle against enemies of the faith, such as experienced by the early Muslim community in its battles with the Meccan pagans. Yet this was not considered the primary meaning. When a troop of Arabs returned from battle boasting of their jihad, the Prophet rebuked them, telling them that they had engaged only in the lesser jihad, of physical battle; the greater jihad was the struggle against one's own baser instincts. Jihad in this sense had great moral prestige, and it was applied metaphorically to a great many meritorious actions.[4] Because of its implication as a struggle for truth and right, however, political leaders inevitably appropriated jihad as a positive symbol to confer legitimacy on their own activities. Under the empire of the early caliphate, jihad became synonymous with the quest for world domination, and jurists were to be found who supported the interpretation that conquest of all non-Islamic realms was a religious duty. A number of legal scholars rejected this notion, however, and argued that jihad in the military sense was justified only in self-defense. Nevertheless, European colonial officials and Orientalists commonly believed that Muslims were inherently disposed to warfare against non-Muslims, insisting that only the extremist position could be authentically Islamic. Anticolonial resistance in the nineteenth century was often characterized as jihad, and fighters against the French, the British, and the Russians called themselves "strugglers for truth" (*mujahid*).

Islam was not the only legitimate system of divine law, however. Since Islamic theology recognized that every people had received a particular revelation and law through their own prophets, there was no problem in acknowledging the existence of different legal systems. In principle, religious minorities in Muslim societies were allowed, or even required, to administer their internal affairs with their own religious and legal systems. Nor did one have to be a Muslim to be virtuous; 'Ali alluded to this when he remarked, "Government can endure with unbelief, but not with injustice."

The notion that there can be different systems of religious ethics needs to be taken seriously. Some commentators argue that there is a universal system of ethics, equivalent to the proclaimed ideals of what is now called Western civilization. Leaving aside the gaps between ethical principles and actual practice, what is most troubling about this assumption is the way it elevates current Euro-American customs and symbols to the status of the ideal. The last great confrontation of European modernity with another religious and ethical tradition took place in the nineteenth century, in relation to Judaism. After the French Revolution, progressive thinkers proposed the emancipation of the Jews from their isolation in ghettoes. It was assumed that integrating Jews into modern society would naturally lead them to cast off their medieval superstition and, in effect, abandon Judaism as irrational. When Jews continued to cling to their religious faith and customs, modern anti-Semitism arose with a vengeance, claiming that it would never be possible for Jews to become true citizens of a modern nation-state. A similar logic of exclusion was directed at Catholics in America, and as late as 1960 it was still questioned whether loyalty to the pope would compromise a president who was a Catholic. To some extent the vague and awkward term "Judaeo-Christian" is an attempt to assert that there are fundamental agreements between Jews and Christians, overlooking the major theological disagreements as well as the history of anti-Semitism (including the Holocaust). Yet to the extent that it still excludes Muslims and others, a Eurocentric ethical system will have a questionable claim to universality; acknowledging difference in religious ethics will be a vital step in creating the conditions for a global civilization.

Greek Philosophy as a Source of Ethics

Alongside the complex of Islamic religious ethics with its reliance on Qur'an and hadith there was an extensive literature on ethics and proper behavior that drew on illustrious examples from pre-Islamic societies, especially Greek philosophy. By the time the Arab empire reached its maximum extension in the ninth century, it had become a cosmopolitan civilization. Conquest of northern Africa and Spain in the west was matched by expansion in the east through Iraq, Anatolia, Persia, and the frontiers of India.

Contrary to a common modern misperception, the new Arab empire was not a religious enterprise; it was a highly efficient mechanism for conquest, in which membership in Arab tribes counted more than religious affiliation. The Arabs were not interested in converting non-Muslims to Islam. Non-Muslim subjects, in lieu of military service, paid an additional tax initially modeled on the Roman and Persian taxes levied on craftsmen; therefore, conversion to Islam would have meant the loss of revenue to the state—never a popular consideration for rulers. The Arab conquerors frequently kept to themselves in separate garrison cities so they would not have to mix with the local populations, and Christian Arabs had shares in the loot of conquest alongside Muslims. When Syrians, Persians, and Egyptians began to express an interest in joining the faith of their conquerors, whether for practical or spiritual reasons, it was at first a baffling issue for Muslim authorities. Many apparently considered that Islam was basically a religion for the Arabs, comparable to Judaism as an ethnically based faith. Conversion to Islam was initially only conceivable through the mechanism of adoption into Arab tribes. In medieval empires, unlike today, ethnicity rather than religion was often a more important marker of identity. While modern writers usually write of Muslim invasions of India, medieval Indian sources only refer to ethnic groups such as Arabs, Baluchs, or Turks, frequently summing up all foreigners as barbarians; it is apparent that Indians had no sense of Islam as an organizing principle behind military incursions. It is only in comparatively recent times, under the pressure of new communal ideologies, that such different groups have been lumped together as Muslims.[5]

At the same time that an Arab Muslim society was being enriched by contact with the ancient cultures of Asia and the Mediterranean, the structure of imperial government introduced the Arabs to the lifestyles and fashions of the Roman caesar and Persian shah. Not only did the Arabs take over the existing Roman and Persian bureaucracies for the collection of agricultural and artisan taxes; they also adopted all the features of royal rule, such as coinage, court ceremony, and keeping up with rival empires. This, of course, meant that there were major institutions in the new Arab empire that owed little to the precedents established during the lifetime of the Prophet. To address the issues faced by the new polity, it was necessary to draw upon the sophisticated civilizations of the ancient world. For ethics and politics, major sources included the animal fables of India, the powerful traditions of Persian kingship, and the philosophical heritage of the Greeks.

Soon after Baghdad was established in 762 C.E. as the capital of the caliphs (from the Arabic word *khalifa*, meaning successor to the Prophet), it played host to schools of translation and scientific research that produced Arabic versions of important Greek philosophical texts. As a result, the wisdom of Aristotle and Plato soon became part of the repertoire of educated people, including the bureaucrats who ran the empire of the caliphate. Within a couple of centuries, numerous works were available in Arabic that drew upon Greek thinking about the relationship between philosophy and religion. Aristotle's ethics was particularly popular, and it is possible to trace a continuous series of writings in Arabic (and, later, in Persian) that develop the Greek thinker's insights into the nature of morality; this philosophical literature on ethics continued to be produced, particularly in the eastern Muslim countries, right up to the dawn of the colonial period in the eighteenth century.[6] The distinctive feature of philosophical ethics was its use of reason rather than pure authority as the standard of justice and right behavior.

An example of the synthesis of Greek philosophical ethics with Islamic values is the *Jalalian Ethics*, written in Persian by the philosopher and prime minister Davani (d. 1502). A glance at his table of contents indicates how Davani integrates the Greek philosophical perspective into his outlook. The text is divided into three sections: ethics proper, economics, and politics. The section on ethics covers topics such as the purification of character, virtues and vices, justice, and the diseases of the soul and their cures. The chapter on economics addresses primarily the concept of domestic management and discusses property, the family, eating and drinking, rights of parents, and service. Under politics, Davani begins like Aristotle with the necessity of life in cities, that is, civilization, together with the institutions of kingship. In this connection he investigates the human need for civilization, the virtues of love, the various types of city, the nature of justice, the manners of kings, the need for charity, and the classes of people, closing with extensive advice from Plato and Aristotle. While Davani frequently quotes from scripture (the Qur'an) and the prophets (particularly Muhammad), the structure of this book differs considerably from the hadith collection described above. Its organization and logic derive from the Greek tradition of ethics and politics, as mediated through centuries of reflection by Muslim thinkers. It takes the form of a "mirror for princes" addressed to a ruler, rather than being a general handbook for religious scholars.

Davani's ethics shows a fascinating interplay between the Greek philosophical tradition and the religious ethics of Islam. This combination can be seen in his extensive discussion of the virtues of the ideal ruler, particularly when it comes to demonstrating the qualities of mercy and forgiveness in time of war:

> As long as it is possible to take a prisoner alive, he should not be killed, for one can conceive of many uses for captives, such as enslavement, gift, or ransom, which can console the hearts of enemies. A Qur'anic text proclaims this: after victory, it is not permitted to kill enemies, except when it is impossible to attain security without killing them. After gaining control, one should not give expression to enmity and fanaticism, for in this situation enemies are property and subjects, and making war on one's own slaves and subjects is contrary

to the principle of justice. It is recorded in the writings of the philosophers that when Alexander, after a victory, did not spare the inhabitants of a city from the sword, Aristotle hastily wrote him a letter to this effect, that if you are excused for killing your enemies before attaining victory, after victory what excuse do you have for killing those who are in your power?

Exercising forgiveness is one of the qualities of the great kings; it brings about a tightly unified realm and solidifies the principles of pomp and magnificence. No matter how great power grows, extending forgiveness makes it more impressive and secure, for it is the means to ensure succession and to secure a glorious order. Someone has said, "If criminals knew what pleasure I take in forgiving, they would present their crimes to me as gifts." In reality, human perfection lies in "being anointed" with the divine attributes, and by reason of the saying "therefore we created them" (Qur'an 11:119), the primordial purpose for the creation of the world and humanity is the manifestation of the real existence of God. God's mercy and forgiveness bring about the splendor of divine manifestation in place of human weakness and defect. It is thus found in the hadith, that if you do not commit sin, God most high will create another group that will commit sin, so that his spontaneous mercy can manifest in the mirror of forgiveness. Therefore divine manifestation in the ornament of forgiveness can be similar to the real origin, which is the source of all good things.[7]

Exhibiting the virtue of forgiveness not only follows the advice of Greek philosophers like Aristotle but also displays one of the essential qualities of God according to the Qur'an. By demonstrating that Islamic ethics was both religious and philosophical, this text also shows how the concept of what is called Western civilization should necessarily include Islam. That is, Muslim thinkers such as Davani clearly drew on both the heritage of Hebrew prophecy and its successors and the writings of the Greek philosophers.

In establishing the importance of Greek philosophy in Islamic civilization, we are stumbling across one of the great areas of selective amnesia about the nature of Western civilization. If one looks at any history of philosophy or history of science until very recently, the standard story began with the ancient Greeks, reached the high point with Plato and Aristotle, and then went into decline in the early Christian era. Generally one chapter provided a cursory glance at the role of the Arabs in translating Greek writings, particularly those of Aristotle. One then learns that European thinkers such as St. Thomas Aquinas first studied philosophy on the basis of these Arabic versions of Aristotle, which Jewish scholars had translated into Latin in medieval Spain. Most authorities stated that Averroes (d. 1198), the last Arab philosopher whose writings were translated into Latin, represented the death knell of philosophy among the Muslims. Yet there were major schools of philosophy in the Muslim east, particularly in Iran, where philosophers such as Mulla Sadra developed original views that included critical reflections on ancient Greek philosophers such as Plato and Aristotle (see fig. 4.1). In a similar way, early textbooks on the history of Islam frequently concluded that by the tenth century, "the gate of independent reasoning was closed" in all fields of Islamic religious thought, leading to an inevitable stultification and decline. Only in recent years has scholarship revealed rich traditions of innovation and ongoing development in fields such as Islamic law in many different regions.

What is most amazing about this concept of civilizational decline, aside from its inaccuracy, is the way it demonstrates a narrowly Eurocentric concept of history. Because no other works of

به بهانه چهارصدوچهلمین سال تولد حکیم ملاصدرا (ره)
همایش جهانی بزرگداشت ، درهفته‌اول
خردادماه درتهران برگزار میگردد.

The World Congress on Mulla Sadra , on the occasion
of his four hundred fortieth birthday,
Tehran-Iran-May 23-27,1999

FIGURE 4.1

Poster showing the Iranian philosopher Mulla Sadra
(d. 1640), arrayed over busts of Socrates, Plato, and
Aristotle (Mulla Sadra Conference, Tehran, 1999)

philosophy were translated from Arabic into Latin after around 1200, Europeans assumed that philosophy was dead among the Arabs. This bold declaration went hand-in-hand with the doctrine that Arab civilization (and Muslim civilization in general) had gone into decline, from which it would only be saved by the arrival of European colonialism. Thus philosophy could be seen as essentially belonging to the legitimate heirs of Western civilization, that is, the western Europeans. The interest of the Arabs in philosophy was considered to be only an interlude in which they preserved philosophy, as if in an icebox, until its true owners could finally take possession during the Renaissance.

The denial of philosophy among Muslims was an argument for European superiority. Such was the contention of Ernst Renan in his surreal debate with Afghani in 1883, when he denied that Semites were capable of philosophy. European scholars actually were aware that Muslims produced philosophical writings in later times (the *Jalalian Ethics* of Davani was available in an English version in 1839), but it is rare to find any reference to this until very recently. It took the efforts of mavericks such as French scholar Henry Corbin (1903–78) to document the existence of highly sophisticated traditions of philosophy, particularly in Iran and India, in the centuries following the death of Averroes.[8] Other scholars have demonstrated that the impact of Greek thought on Islamic civilization went far beyond the limited circles of specialists who studied philosophical texts. Simply considered as a powerful system for organizing thought and logic and as a medium for debate, Greek philosophy acted as a leavening agent leading to new results in fields as varied as Arabic grammar, rhetoric, theology, and principles of jurisprudence. Greek logicians (Porphyry) and mathematicians (Euclid) continued to be part of the curriculum of study in many Muslim countries until relatively recent times. Yet somehow Islam continues to be viewed as alien to the Western heritage.

Europeans are hardly the only ones who have exercised ethnocentrism in their concepts of civilization and culture. Indians, Chinese, and Arabs have all been guilty of similar conceits in the past. But it is the modern European self-image that dominates the concept that we have all inherited of what constitutes civilization, and therefore it is the concept that needs to be examined most carefully. One only needs to glance at any American college or university department of philosophy to realize that the dominant concept of philosophy is almost entirely European, a secular product of the Enlightenment. The standard philosophy curriculum begins with the ancient Greeks and gives a brief nod to medieval Christian thinkers, but it concentrates on modern enlightened Europeans (and Americans) from the time of Descartes (d. 1650) to the present. From our modern educational curriculum, one would never guess that there are provocative and original philosophical thinkers in majority Muslim countries as well as in other parts of Asia and Africa. By defining civilization so narrowly as to include only Europeans and Americans, we relegate the rest of the world to barbarism. Yet this Eurocentric attitude can only be maintained through selective amnesia about the rest of the world.

Islamic Ethics in the Colonial Age

The age of European colonial rule was, as previously remarked, a watershed in the history of Muslim countries. How did Muslim approaches to ethics change as a result of this momentous period? One of the effects of colonial rule was the suspension of local legal systems (including any aspects of Islamic *shari'a* law) and the imposition of the law of the conqueror. In the French dominions it was the Code Napoleon, in British possessions it was the common law, and in Russian territories it was Czarist law (superseded by Soviet law after the Russian Revolution). Although European commercial and criminal codes took decisive effect, the new legal systems were not complete replacements; local custom persisted in many aspects of life, and the conquerors felt reluctant to intrude too deeply into family law for fear of unnecessarily encouraging resistance. The result was the creation of composite systems of family law, such as Anglo-Mohammedan law in British India. In matters of marriage, divorce, and inheritance, the court drew on classical Islamic legal texts, which were interpreted by British judges in English translations with the advice of native scholars. In places such as Egypt, where the French and the British ruled in succession, the structure of the law drew on more than one European code. The result was in some cases a much more rigid interpretation of Islamic law than had previously been customary. Examination of court records in Egypt before and during the colonial period indicates that women tended to be much more excluded from access to the law under European rule. Moreover, European judges made rulings on issues such as domestic violence that eroded rights that had been available to Muslim women previously.[9]

Another result of European conquest and colonialism was the overthrow of local elites, the dismantling of existing patronage networks, and the consequent impoverishment of traditional philanthropy, including education. In practical terms, this meant that nineteenth-century Muslim educational institutions were forced to retrench their advanced offerings and fall back on a core curriculum focusing on scripture. One example would be northern India, where a scholar named Nizam al-Din established around 1700 a curriculum of Islamic education aimed at training officials for the bureaucracy of the Mughal Empire. This "Nizami curriculum" (*dars-i Nizami*), which closely resembled curricula then found in the Ottoman and Persian regions, emphasized the rational sciences, including logic, theology, and philosophy. It soon spread throughout South Asia, becoming the standard form of Islamic education in India in the nineteenth century. Although the name Nizami curriculum continues to appear in many academies today, the content has changed drastically, due to the elimination of the rational sciences.

Major changes in Muslim education took place after the British suppressed an Indian revolt in 1857, eliminating the last vestiges of Muslim political power. Classical forms of Islamic education were now irrelevant to a successful career in government, since English had become necessary for entry into service with the British. The traditional higher curriculum in rational sciences accordingly faded away, and the new Islamic religious academies established in the colonial period had a very different perspective. The study of the hadith of Muhammad became the core of the curriculum in the new religious academy of Deoband (founded in 1867), which had as its mission not the training of elite bureaucrats but the formation of a pious community. The founders of Deoband no longer sought support from the state (which was not Islamic in any case) but from the public instead. The new technology of print became the medium for distributing authoritative religious texts on a mass basis, and the spread of literacy under the British colonial state encouraged this transformation. In earlier times, Islamic academies had been small institutions without formal organization, with individualized instruction, but the new institutions had their eye on British models, with fixed multiyear curricula and elaborate bureaucratic structures.

With the newly authoritarian emphasis on modeling one's behavior on the Prophet, the Deoband teachers became the vanguard of reformist Muslim thinking in South Asia and the center of an immense network of spin-off academies. For Deobandis, ethics consisted of following the Prophet Muhammad in every conceivable detail. They implemented their ethical judgment by disseminating their legal opinions (*fatwas*) throughout the South Asian subcontinent, in response to questions from the Muslim community. Because of their strongly textual focus on hadith, they tended to condemn any local customs that were not accounted for in these early authoritative sources. This meant that they criticized many popular practices, such as elaborate wedding customs, excessive veneration of the Prophet or Sufi saints, and any of the ritual practices associated with Shi'ism. They also emphasized the seclusion of women as a sign of a moral society, although they favored education for women, particularly religious education in their own doctrines.

What is new in the Islamic ethics of Deoband? It is not simply a question of which texts are being used, but the overall orientation—which means the contemporary context. Using hadith texts that ultimately derive from the time of the Prophet does not actually transport students back 1,400 years. The new religious academies operate in the shadow of the modern secular state, whether colonial or postcolonial. They use the authority of scriptural texts to establish their own role as interpreters of tradition, addressing a host of distinctively modern problems brought to their attention by the community of the faithful. While religious teachers have always made claims to authority, the bureaucratic organization and mass distribution of primary scriptural texts in the new academies is a distinctively modern experience, with the organization of ideological political parties plus an argumentative technique similar to that of Christian missionaries. Within South Asia, the nominally secular government of India has adopted a hands-off attitude toward leading academies such as Deoband, but governments of the officially Islamic republics of Pakistan and Bangladesh have not been able to refrain from meddling with these institutions. Partly this is from the modernist impulse to make traditional academies more useful to society by adding "practical" subjects to their curricula. But, in part, postcolonial Muslim countries are faced with a severe crisis over the concept of the Islamic state. Although the ethics of Deoband do not seem to call for any particular political model (leaders of this school opposed the creation of Pakistan and remained in secular India), once a so-called Islamic state is established, it becomes a central issue defining Muslim identity.

The End of the Caliphate and the Concept of the Islamic State

While the example of Deoband is only one of the many Islamic movements that have arisen during modern times, it, like the rest, is framed by the twin experiences of European colonialism and the rise of the modern nation-state. The superior firepower of European military technology eliminated local dynasties throughout Asia and Africa. One of the last arenas of conflict was the Ottoman Empire, which held sway over the eastern Mediterranean and parts of southeastern Europe. Rising European commercial and military power was able to extract advantageous concessions and legal immunities from the Ottomans for Europeans and for Christian minorities within the empire, through formal treaties. These forced agreements, summarized under headings ("capitula"), were known as the Ottoman capitulations, thus giving that term the meaning of a complete surrender of sovereignty.

The ruling institution of the Ottomans was technically known as the sultanate, but the sultans also claimed a religious office, the caliphate, or succession to the authority of the

Prophet Muhammad. This was a historical anachronism, since the last actual dynasty that claimed this title, the 'Abbasids, had been wiped out by Mongol invaders in 1258. After that time, political theorists extended the courtesy title of caliph to any Muslim ruler who protected Islamic religious practice and institutions. The Ottomans, however, adopted the title of caliph with a distinctly religious pretension, in a treaty signed with the Russians in 1774; in a novel interpretation, they claimed through this mechanism a kind of political jurisdiction over Muslims living in the Russian Empire. Now in a rearguard effort to reclaim some kind of religious authority over other Muslims, the last Ottoman sultans attempted to play the card of caliph, even as their political power was waning.

The grandiose plans of Sultan 'Abd al-Hamid II (r. 1876–1909) to create a pan-Islamic movement under his own leadership foundered on a many-leveled crisis. The concept of nationalism, based on European models, spread rapidly through the Ottoman Empire at the beginning of the twentieth century, creating a new Turkish nationalist movement (the "Young Turks") as well as nationalist movements among minorities such as Armenians. The uncompromising loyalty demanded by nationalism became a divisive force that eventually helped tear the empire apart. The Ottoman defeat in World War I was the decisive blow; not only were the Balkan and Near Eastern provinces lost, but there were four European armies on Turkish soil. The secular nationalist leader Mustafa Kemal Ataturk ("father of the Turks") expelled the invaders and proclaimed Turkey a secular republic in 1922, abolishing the office of the sultan and most of the religious institutions of the empire. But the former sultan still retained the purely symbolic title of caliph, which became a powerful symbol of vanished power among Muslims around the world. Tiring of special pleading on the caliph's behalf by foreign Muslims, Ataturk in 1924 decided to abolish the office of the caliphate as well. The chief symbol of international Islamic sovereignty had ceased to exist.

Although the meaning of the caliphate under the Ottomans was questionable, the extinction of this symbolic office raised the issue of politics among Muslims with unprecedented urgency. Although none of the nominally Muslim dynasties ruling in Africa and Asia were particularly religious governments, their nearly total defeat by European, Russian, and Chinese forces was seen as a blow to Islam. While colonial rulers pontificated about the civilizational decline of Muslims as a justification for conquest, reformist Muslim thinkers accepted this argument, but with a twist. In their view, it was not an intrinsic defect in Islamic civilization that had led to the decline of Muslim nations; it was, rather, the failure of Muslims to live by God's commands that had caused their defeat. From this tragic situation, tailor-made for a preacher, arose the new concept of the Islamic state, which has now become a principal concern of many contemporary Muslim thinkers. After this point, reformist Muslims began to redefine Islam as the ideology that is the basis of the Islamic state.

The initial mobilization of Islamist groups in colonial India and Egypt did not start auspiciously. In the 1920s and 1930s, Hasan al-Banna organized the Muslim Brotherhood in Egypt, and in 1941, Abu al-'Ala' Maudoodi founded the Jama'at-i Islami (Islamic Society) in India. As the prototypes for all later so-called fundamentalist groups, these organizations employed the reformist rhetoric of claiming to return to the original and pristine form of the Islamic faith. This strategy was also designed to discredit rival Islamic leaders, on the grounds that they represented corrupt deviations from the true path. Maudoodi and Hasan al-Banna were, nevertheless, thoroughly modern (neither was trained in a traditional Islamic academy), and both were squarely placed in anticolonial resistance.

Nevertheless, the Islamist parties did not do well politically at the ballot box, and they did not appear to have mass followings. But the eventual retreat of colonial powers seemed to offer new opportunities for authority in the postcolonial states (although Maudoodi, ironically, opposed the creation of the state of Pakistan, on the grounds that it would create division in the worldwide Islamic "nation"). The new leaders of independent states were, however, socialists and secularists, and they efficiently seized the levers of the centralized power bequeathed them by their colonial predecessors. So began the tradition of one-party rule and presidency for life that has been all too typical for postcolonial governments around the world (whether Muslim or non-Muslim). In Egypt, Socialist leader Gamal Abdel Nasser suppressed the Muslim Brotherhood after members attempted to assassinate him, and he had its leaders imprisoned and executed. Military rulers in Algeria and Tunisia have also persecuted organized Islamist parties. Reformist Islam was basically arrayed against the modern nation-state.

Generalizations about Islamic politics, even if focused on reformist movements, have to be extensively qualified in terms of the context that matters most: the individual nation-state.[10] Nevertheless, insofar as postcolonial regimes have usually shared the same problems of lack of democratic representation and inequitable distribution of resources, reformist political groups have generally positioned themselves similarly in Muslim majority countries. One of the only public spaces that secular regimes cannot control is the mosque, and Friday prayer sermons are the occasions when it is most possible to criticize repressive governments. In addition, Islamist groups like the Muslim Brotherhood in Egypt and Hamas among Palestinians sometimes provide people with major social services, such as education and health, which governments have failed to make available. As is the case with Jewish and Christian fundamental-

ists in other countries, Islamists vehemently criticize the elimination of God from governments and the public space. It is their
feeling that all of life should be ordered according to God's command, in this way eliminating the sins and weaknesses to which
human decisions are prone. Those who wish to erect the Ten
Commandments in American courthouses are operating on
premises similar to those of Islamic reformists.

Yet the antisecular politics of the proponents of the Islamic
state by no means exhaust the possibilities of religiously based
social activism in Muslim societies. Nongovernmental organizations like the Grameen Bank in Bangladesh and the Eidhi
Foundation in Pakistan make available social services such as
microcredit lending and health services for the indigent. Based
on both traditional Muslim notions of charity and more recent
concepts of development and education, these modern organizations provide homegrown methods for addressing social
problems.

The dream of an Islamic state is often more powerful when it
remains vague and unspecified. An anecdote from prerevolu-
tionary Iran illustrates how the appeal of Islam was presented as
the universal solution. Tehran is a city that expanded far beyond
its planned infrastructure, due to the migration of millions of
people from rural areas over the past few decades. One of the
results is that there is still a system of open sewers alongside
streets, which can be a disgusting experience, particularly if one
loses one's footing. During the last years of the Shah's reign,
someone was overheard complaining bitterly about the sewers.
"Don't worry," replied a listener, "that will be taken care of—by
Islam." Although the speaker probably had no specific connection in mind that would stretch from classical Islamic texts to
the installation of new sewer systems, the remark illustrates how
the solution to all modern problems can be sought from Islam.

Examples of Islam and the Modern State in Practice

Given the decisive impact of colonialism on Islamic political thought, it is interesting to look at the political character of the four Muslim countries that technically did not come under complete colonial rule, that is, Turkey, Saudi Arabia, Afghanistan, and Iran. Each of these countries over the past century has had a markedly distinct political history. Turkey became a secular nationalist state in which Islam happens to be the majority religion but is theoretically denied any major role in government. Saudi Arabia continues to be an Arab tribal monarchy that survives on the basis of oil wealth and through its strong alliance with a puritanical sect, the Wahhabis. Afghanistan in 1921 adopted a constitutional monarchy whose authority sat lightly upon a complicated patchwork of different ethnic groups, within boundaries drawn by the British after three wars in the nineteenth century; a Soviet-backed Marxist government took power in 1978, only to be dethroned by mujahideen resistance in 1992, followed in 1996 by the theocratic tribal movement of the Taliban. The lack of uniformity among these national experiences reveals the debatable nature of the politics of the Islamic state. The case of Afghanistan, which is currently the most notorious due to the American overthrow of the Taliban in 2002, vividly illustrates how intrusion by foreign powers has played a decisive role in that nation's destiny.

Iran is, however, the most fascinating example of the application of Islamic political theory in recent years, although it should be stressed again that no Muslim country particularly acts as a paradigm for others—national history is always distinctive. Saddled with a weak monarchy, in the nineteenth century Iran balanced uneasily between the aggressive power of the Russians to the north and the British coming from the Persian Gulf and from India. In 1906 a constitutional revolution took place that introduced a democratic assembly, but within a few years the Shah (assisted by a Russian-trained Cossack brigade) closed down the parliament. After Iran was occupied by European forces in World War I, an Iranian Cossack officer took power in 1921 and soon named himself Shah, though the Russians and the British overthrew him in 1942 for siding with the Nazis. But when a democratically elected government threatened to nationalize the oil industry in 1953, U.S. intelligence operatives (the Central Intelligence Agency) overthrew the government and installed Muhammad Reza Shah as king. Iran's close military and economic dependence on the United States led to treaties in the 1960s that granted Americans and their dependents full exemption from Iranian law. These agreements, which closely resembled the Ottoman capitulations of the nineteenth century, drew outraged protests from Muslim religious authorities, who saw them as a complete abdication of national sovereignty. Opposition grew under the leadership of the exiled Ayatollah Khomeini, and a combination of government oppression and corruption eventually provoked the revolution of 1978–79 and the overthrow of the Shah.

Although the Iranian revolution was carried out by a combination of Islamic and secular forces, it was Ayatollah Khomeini who set up the blueprint for the national government now known as the Islamic Republic of Iran. His theory of government, though couched in classical religious texts, was very much a product of the twentieth century. Khomeini at times emphasized a socialist perspective on economics, and he consistently maintained an anticolonial view of national sovereignty. The model of government to emerge from the revolution, as out-lined in the 1979 constitution on the basis of Khomeini's ideas, is also in many ways a very modern concept.[11] The Iranian revolution is described as based on an ideological and Islamic movement against colonialism (see fig. 5.2 for a graphic revolutionary image using an Islamic slogan). Government is divided into legislative, executive, and judicial branches, and it is worth noting that recent elections have successfully drawn the participation of a large part of the electorate. The government's goals include favoring morality, developing the mass media, supporting education and research, opposing imperialism and despotism, advancing freedom within the law, securing public participation in policy, abolishing discrimination, attaining efficiency in government, eliminating discrimination, providing economic justice, advancing scientific and technological sufficiency, supporting citizens' rights, and strengthening Islamic brotherhood internally and internationally. Women's rights and the rights of religious minorities are also carefully spelled out in this document. Much of this would be expected to appear in the constitution of any modern nation.

What is at first surprising, though, is the large role that religion plays in the Iranian constitution. There is an official state religion, which is Shi'i Islam, and religious authority is vested in a Guardian Council of judges having veto power over legislation. Khomeini's boldest innovation was his theory of "the Guardian Jurist," who has ultimate authority over the nation; the authority of this supreme leader in political terms is theoretically equivalent to that of the Prophet or his twelve successors, the Imams. Yet on closer examination, a predominant national religion is not all that unusual in the world today. There are a number of nations that have an official religion or that require the head of state to practice a particular faith. In practice, the Islamic Republic of Iran can be compared to the Jewish state of Israel in terms of religion as a decisive factor. While Israel lacks a formal constitution stipulating the legal status of religion, candidates for the Israeli parliament are required to accept the notion that Israel is a Jewish state, and Jewish religious parties exert an influence far greater than their numerical strength, particularly when the major parties are evenly balanced. But in either case, the language that proclaims religion as the source of the principles of the state is in a very important sense deceptive, because it is the state that makes that declaration, and so it is the state that authorizes religion, rather than the other way around. In practice, Islam in Iran is defined by the supreme leader and the small group of men who comprise the Guardian Council.

Liberal Islam

The foregoing remarks on the concept of the Islamic state should not be taken to mean that reformist Islam has a monopoly, or even necessarily a dominant role, in modern Muslim thinking on ethics and politics. This is far from being the case, although the news media have typically seized upon the most extreme examples of Muslim reformism (known as fundamentalism or Islamism), due to their sensational and confrontational character. One of the chief alternatives to reformism over the past century is often known as liberal Islam, and this concept, as one scholar observes, is not a contradiction in terms.[12] Indeed, from the late 1800s onward, Muslims from every part of Africa and Asia were aware of the debates that agitated Europeans, although too often this information came through colonial channels that did not consider the "natives" to be on an equal footing.

In the earliest stage of liberal Islam, modernist Muslims

worked toward the formation or reformation of educational institutions, argued for political liberalization or decolonization, and attempted to establish newspapers and periodicals to express their views. In the twentieth century the key goals for liberal Muslims were democracy, freedom of thought and religion, women's rights, and human rights in general. It should also be acknowledged that socialism and Marxism have played extremely important roles in a number of Muslim countries, particularly the Arab countries. While liberalism certainly has its critics in Muslim countries, it is remarkable that Europeans and Americans sometimes dismiss liberal Muslim thinkers as irrelevant, evidently because of a habitual tendency to regard only Muslim fundamentalism as true Islam. For example, people ask whether Islam can coexist with democracy. The question is unusual, not only because it appears to dismiss the democratic aspirations of millions of Muslims over the past century and longer, but also because it assumes that other religions such as Christianity are (unlike Islam) compatible with democracy. One should recall that democracy does not have much of a profile in the history of Christianity, but that it belongs instead to the modern Enlightenment together with the separation of church and state. This is another example of how media-driven stereotypes reinforce fundamentalism; ironically, this process turns non-Muslims into supporters of fundamentalism, as they adopt a narrow interpretation of Islam even (and especially) when they are criticizing Islamist groups.

Although one cannot completely separate modern Islam from colonialism, it would be a mistake to argue that either liberal or reformist Islam is a reflexive response to European ideas. Many of the most sophisticated modernist and liberal Muslim thinkers were quite aware of the complex and rich heritage of ethical and political thinking in earlier Muslim tradition. For these thinkers, "ethical questions . . . must take into account the diversity and pluralism that has marked the Muslims of the past as well as the present."[13] Early schools of Islamic theology, such as the rationalist school known as the Mu'tazila, argued that the Qur'an mandates reason as a standard for interpreting revelation. Contemporary thinkers such as the Indonesian theologian Harun Nasution have revived this rationalist perspective, viewing the Qur'an as a necessary source of basic moral themes but not as the final blueprint for human society imagined by Islamists.[14]

Likewise, contemporary Iranian philosopher Abdul-Karim Soroush has come under severe criticism and repression from elements of the Iranian government due to his contention that absolute religion exists only for God, while in the human sphere there are multiple interpretations of religion. He maintains that the achievement of premodern Islamic philosophers like Mulla Sadra (d. 1640) was "a reinterpretation of shari'a [Islamic law] according to the principles of philosophy, that is, to subsume it under philosophical categories."[15] Thinkers such as Soroush argue against authoritarian Islamists in favor of pluralism, and they use both Islamic scriptural texts and the extensive Islamic theological and philosophical tradition; they are also thoroughly familiar with modern European philosophers, from Kant and Hegel to those of the present day. Unfortunately, due to the massive cultural amnesia about the non-European world that is the by-product of globalization, nearly all these modern Muslim thinkers remain unknown even to the highly educated in Europe and America. As long as we are not able even to hear the voices of these thinkers, we will not be able to have a genuine dialogue of civilizations.

Gender and the Question of Veiling

According to the traditions of Shi'i Muslims, the revolt of Imam Husayn against the tyrannical Caliph Yazid in 680 C.E. ended in the greatest tragedy in the history of Islam. Not only was the Prophet's grandson killed along with his male followers, but the women of his family were stripped of their veils and paraded publicly in disgrace. Brought to the presence of the caliph in Damascus, Husayn's sister Zaynab remained defiant, openly challenging Yazid's authority and lamenting the death of her brother, who was the rightful inheritor of the authority of the Prophet. So striking was her indignation that the caliph was shamed and let her and the others depart in peace.[16]

This dramatic picture, which has been evoked by many poems of lamentation, presents a powerful reminder of the important roles played by women in the early Muslim community. Women have never been ciphers or nonentities in Islamic history. The wives of the Prophet Muhammad were his partners and supporters in the creation of the new society, and they continued to have eminence after his death. 'A'isha is noteworthy for transmitting more than 2,000 hadith reports from the Prophet (although only about 300 of these were retained in the principal collections), and she was the principal leader of an unsuccessful revolt against 'Ali. The prominence of women in early Muslim society stands in contrast with the image of Muslim women today, at least as they are perceived in Europe and America. The standard picture of the Muslim woman shows someone who is oppressed by men, restricted to home, and veiled in public, although this image is admittedly anonymous and not related to any particular location. The extraordinary recent behavior of the Taliban in Afghanistan, who denied women education and even the most basic rights, has encouraged the impression that Islam is dedicated to the oppression of women. How can we reconcile these conflicting depictions of Muslim women?

As mentioned earlier, Islamic law in theory provides resources for women, such as property rights, which were not available to European women until very recent times. Yet in practice the complex application of Islamic law was filtered through multiple levels of custom and tradition, so that ethical principles of equality between the sexes all too frequently were sacrificed for the benefit of male privilege. The imposition of patriarchal authority over women is hardly unique to Islamic civilization. Aristotle, it must be remembered, regarded women as natural slaves. Despite statements about gender equality in the New Testament, there are also strong traditions that for centuries have excluded women from positions of authority in Christian churches. Misogyny and the assertion of men's authority over women is, in fact, characteristic of the history of much of the world, including China and India. Disentangling the roles of the ethics of gender and patriarchal history is a task that now is being undertaken in every culture, even when it does not bear the name of feminism.

What makes the discussion of gender relations in Islamic cultures especially tricky is, once again, the effects of European colonialism.[17] By the late nineteenth century, Europeans had developed a number of arguments to demonstrate the cultural inferiority of the nations of the Orient, principally Muslim countries. As mentioned previously, the scientific language of racial categories and the alleged evolutionary superiority of Europeans were key elements in the ideology of colonial ascendancy. A new and surprising weapon in the colonialists' arsenal was the language of European feminism. However uncomfortable Victorian officials may have been with feminist agitation for equal rights at home, they eagerly and hypocritically criticized Asian and especially Muslim men for their bad treatment of women (although some colonial administrators, such as Lord Cromer and Lord Curzon, were active opponents of the British suffragette movement). By maintaining that Islam was essentially oppressive to women and by linking Muslim backwardness to the practice of veiling women, colonial administrators could justify their rule over Asia and Africa, since they were the bearers of enlightened modernity. At the same time, they maintained that Muslims could only become civilized if they abandoned veiling—that is, if they abandoned what were believed to be essential practices of Islam. The same rhetoric of condescending shock about the veiling of Muslim women continues to be applied today, despite less than perfect gender equity in Europe and America.

When we look, however, at the authoritative Islamic scriptures, we can see prominent resources for an ethic of gender equality. In Christian and Jewish circles, it is only in relatively recent years that the gendered language of the Bible has become an issue, leading to new translations that do not automatically assume the male gender as normal. Yet gender-specific language had clearly become a concern in the early Muslim community. A number of women approached the Prophet Muhammad to ask him about the prevalence of male pronouns in the Qur'an, wanting to know if women were included in these statements. The next revelations of the Qur'an responded directly to these concerns, with an extended series of balanced phrases that make it clear that men and women share equally in the religious life:

> For the submitting men and submitting women,
> for the believing men and the believing women,
> for the devout men and the devout women,

for the sincere men and the sincere women,
for the patient men and the patient women,
for the humble men and the humble women,
for the men and the women who give alms,
for the men and the women who fast,
for the men and the women who guard their chastity,
and for the men and the women who remember God
   much—
for them God has prepared forgiveness and a great reward.
   (33:35)

It would be hard to find another example of a major scripture that addresses the issue of gender language so specifically. In another section of the Qur'an, God specifically regards the acts of men and women as of equal worth: "I do not neglect the deeds done by any of you, whether man or woman; the one of you comes from the other" (3:195).

Nonetheless, the Qur'an also contains general injunctions about modesty for both men and women as well as specific observations aimed at the wives of the Prophet. Hadith reports contain more extensive accounts of the situations that led up to the revelation of certain verses.[18] The precise extent to which these verses are authoritative for later situations is unclear. For instance, when Muhammad celebrated his wedding to Zaynab, some male guests stayed late, annoying the Prophet by intruding too long in the women's quarters. This led to the proclamation of a Qur'anic verse stating, "When you ask them [the Prophet's wives] for something, ask them from behind a curtain" (33:53). This "curtain" (*hijab*) is the beginning point for the concept of veiling, but at this time it applied to the wives of the Prophet in a very special sense. They were singled out in the Qur'an, as in the verse cited above, and they were specifically described as being unlike other women—including the special requirement that they could not remarry after the Prophet's death. There was, however, no distinctive female garb dictated by the Qur'an, only a general instruction that women should dress modestly and cover their breasts (24:31).

Major changes took place in Muslim society, however, after the imperial conquests of the next generation. It was especially when Arab armies overran the territories of the eastern Roman Empire and Persia that they were exposed to sophisticated civilizations that had elaborate customs of seclusion of women and large harems with concubines for the emperor. This was a far cry from the simple society of Arabia in the time of the Prophet. Muhammad, after all, had had a single concubine but no servants, and he was used to repairing his own clothes. The empire of the caliphate was exposed to wealth on an enormous scale, and individual male Arabs were able to own numerous female slaves. Increasingly, religious behavior for Muslim women was modeled on the customs of upper-class Persian, Greek, Roman, and Jewish women, who wore veils so they would be spared the ogling of men in the street. This is a case in which religious behavior imitated social status. The veil that initially was a curtain separating the wives of the Prophet gradually became identified with the concealing clothing worn by all respectable women, particularly in the cities.

In practice there is no single thing that is identifiable as "the veil" in Muslim societies today, nor is veiling synonymous with covering the face. Before the beginning of the colonial period, the clothing that Christian and Jewish women wore in countries such as Egypt was no different from the clothing of Muslim women; only later in the nineteenth century did women from religious minorities in Muslim countries begin to dress in European fashions. If one visits different countries with Muslim majority populations today, it is immediately apparent that women wear different types of clothing in all of these nations. Economic class, urban or rural location, education, and custom lead to a wide range of women's clothing, which may or may not have any religious meaning. The Iranian chador, an all-encompassing black garment without fastenings, can now be replaced by a raincoat and a headscarf called a manteau (the name is actually French). Women in Iran are required to wear one of these options in public, and they are forbidden to apply facial makeup. The chador is not the same as the black *abaya* worn by women of Arabia, and there are many particular tribal variations on nomadic Arab dress. What counts as respectable fashion for Muslim women in West Africa may include colorful wraps and a bare midriff, while observant Southeast Asian Muslim women prefer white headscarves and long dresses. Clothing styles for women in Turkey range from totally European fashion in Istanbul to conservative tribal costumes in rural provinces, although official secularism forbids Islamic headscarves in universities and government offices. Pushtun women in Afghanistan, following local tribal code, wear all-enveloping *burqas*, and their husbands boast that their women observe "the veil and four walls," that is, total seclusion. Yet none of these can be described as a norm that defines Muslim women anywhere else.

Sometimes official attempts to define Islamic dress for women result in strange incongruities. When the Pakistani ruler Gen. Zia ul-Haqq attempted to enforce a program of Islamization in the 1980s, he declared that the Indian sari was not acceptable in government offices and that Islamic dress for women should be the *shalwar kamis* (a long shirt worn over drawstring pants) with a *dupatta* scarf over the head. This is, of course, a typical regional clothing style of northern India and Pakistan worn by men and women without regard to religion. Yet by decree of the state, it was defined as Islamic clothing. Such was the weight attached to these clothing styles that astute observers of the Pakistani political scene swore they could correlate conservative and liberal trends in government by interpreting the position of the female newscaster's headscarf on Pakistan television (full coverage of hair by the scarf indicated conservatism, but loose pulling back of the scarf or allowing it to drop to the shoulders were clear signs of relaxation in the regime).

The definition of particular women's clothing as Islamic owes much to anticolonial sentiments; before the arrival of European conquerors, it was just seen as what women normally wore. While European colonial administrators saw the veil as a sign of Islamic backwardness, in recent years this interpretation has been challenged; there has been a new ideological emphasis on veiling among Muslim women in countries such as Egypt and Turkey. While their mothers and grandmothers had cheerfully adopted European-style dress and cast aside head coverings, women in the 1980s began to adopt the veil to demonstrate their anti-Western nationalism. Covering also became a sign of their resistance to the immoral use of women's bodies in advertising by multinational companies. It is striking that the two pieces of plain seamless cloth that constitute the official garment for women performing the hajj to Mecca leave the face unveiled. Evidently the egalitarian spirit of this enormous meeting of believers would be in conflict with the aristocratic attitude that calls for veiling the face.

These variations in women's dress raise the question of Muslim women's perspectives and how Muslim women express themselves to reclaim their own tradition. What is at first surprising to many Americans and Europeans is that Muslim women have voices at all. Here, too, there are many examples with which to counter this amnesia and inattention, and the record goes back many years. Early-twentieth-century Muslim feminists, including a number of male authors, resembled early European and American feminists in their emphasis on domesticity, education, and hygiene, stressing the important role of women in rearing the next generation. In many countries Muslim women of the upper class established a tradition of founding schools devoted to the education of girls. By the 1920s, feminist authors in Syria and Egypt had created organizations, led public demonstrations, and written books criticizing patriarchal interpretations of Islam. In 1928 Lebanese feminist Nazira Zayn al-Din wrote *Unveiling and Veiling*, a book that caused an immense sensation due to her insistence that men had misinterpreted veiling as a religious requirement.[19] The strategy of Islamic feminists is quite similar to the approach of Christian and Jewish feminists, although many Muslim women prefer to avoid the label of "feminist," since it is often associated with European colonialism and anti-Islamic attitudes. The original scriptural sources can be scrutinized critically by women as well as by men, and it is particularly important to reexamine the ways in which male scholars have interpreted them. Thus Moroccan feminist author Fatima Mernissi decided to reexamine hadith in which the Prophet had allegedly declared that women were unfit to govern. She could not believe that a man who was so respectful and considerate of women during his life could have made such a negative remark. Using techniques of traditional Islamic scholarship on hadith, she found reasons to question the credibility of the chief transmitter of this report, who seems to have been biased against the Prophet's wife 'A'isha.[20] This is a way in which Muslim feminist scholars have questioned male-dominated interpretation by engaging directly with authoritative scriptural texts.

This is not to say that Muslim majority societies do not have problems in the modern implementation of family law.[21] There are fierce debates taking place on these issues in every country, and those debates are extraordinarily important not only for the actual welfare of women but also for the changing interpretations of Islamic law. There are also serious controversies today among Muslims over homosexuality, just as in Europe and America among Christians. Regarding women's rights, among the mullahs who have run the Islamic Republic of Iran since 1979, there are feminist thinkers who argue for the equality of men and women before the law, using the resources of Islamic jurisprudence as a basis.[22] Iranian authorities in recent years have implemented a remarkably thorough family planning policy based on contraception and vasectomies that has been very effective in reducing the birthrate. Much-debated issues in Muslim countries include the (still infrequent) practice of multiple wives, divorce procedures, abortion, and laws governing rape and adultery. Postcolonial governments have struggled with the reconciliation of Muslim personal law with the broader notion of a uniform civil code for all citizens, regardless of religion. One of the most highly contested recent cases in India revolved around the issue of maintenance for a divorced Muslim woman named Shahbano. Non-Muslim judges settled her case with a narrow ruling that awarded her a pittance, based on the complex colonial code of Anglo-Mohammedan law. The case aroused the ire of secularists and Hindus who objected to the state paying such deference to Islamic law, and it also drew massive protests from Muslims who feared that the Indian state would interfere with Islam. There are, in addition, problems arising from tribal customs such as "honor killings," which are the result of murderous vengeance directed at women who are considered to have shamed their families by inappropriate behavior. Another issue is clitoridectomy, or female genital mutilation, an ancient practice found mainly in certain regions of Africa. In the Nile Valley about 70 percent of Muslims and nearly 100 percent of Christians follow this practice, and it is also widespread in Sudan and Western Africa among followers of traditional religions. These practices do not derive from Islamic law but are instances of conflict between Islamic *shari'a* and local custom.

Despite the challenges that women face in different Muslim societies, it is important for Europeans and Americans to avoid treating them with condescension, with the assumption that Islam is a prison from which Muslim women seek to be liberated. As mentioned previously, this kind of critique of Muslim attitudes toward women has been a significant element in the justification of colonialism, and it ignores the serious gender issues that exist in Euro-American societies. This condescension is deeply resented by the millions of Muslim women who insist on their Muslim identity, even as they struggle with the same issues that women face around the world: maintaining family life alongside increasing economic demands on women, dealing with control of fertility, and seeking an authentic understanding of their rights as women. Moreover, it is worth noting that women in Muslim societies frequently have access to women's social networks based on but going beyond extended family, which can be hard to find in the more atomized societies of Europe and America. There are, in addition, local traditions of women's religious practice, such as the women's mosques of China, that offer opportunities for Muslim women that would never be expected on the basis of stereotypes and generalities.[23] As the example of Zaynab shows, Muslim women should not be underestimated.

Islam and Science

As indicated previously, Islamic civilization was home to a complex of traditions that included not only divine revelation but also human reasoning, particularly through the disciplines associated with Greek philosophy. One of the typical divisions of knowledge among classical Arabic authors classified all subjects into two categories: the traditional sciences, which were authoritative fields of knowledge based on religion and historical tradition, and the rational sciences, in which advances could continually be made. Unlike modern philosophy, which restricts itself to a range of theoretical problems such as theories of knowledge and philosophy of mind, philosophy in Muslim cultures (known in Arabic as *falsafa*) went hand in hand with a full range of practical scientific disciplines, with special emphasis on astronomy and medicine. In part, this emphasis on science was due to the requirements of job security, for many philosophers earned their livelihood by acting as consulting physicians and astrologers in the employment of kings. The sciences of medicine and astronomy in this way had immediate practical relevance to patrons of philosophy. But the ancient philosophical tradition going back to Aristotle had always included disciplined and critical thinking about mathematics and the natural world. The continuation of ancient scientific tradition in Islamicate societies was therefore a natural accompaniment to philosophical tradition, and it was one in which scientists of various religious backgrounds (Muslim, Christian, Jewish, Hindu, and pagan) participated.[24]

The pursuit of scientific knowledge among Muslims was not based on purely external considerations, however. Because of ritual requirements, such as the five daily prayers and the stipulation that one face Mecca, Muslims needed to expand beyond the simple astronomical observations and lunar calendar of the pre-Islamic Arabs. Royal patrons thus had religious motives for sponsoring astronomical observatories and the compilation of tables of observations of planets and stars (see fig. 4.2).[25] From the early ninth century, research in Muslim countries incorporated materials from Indian, Greek, and Persian traditions of astronomical observation and theory, with the geocentric Ptole-maic system of planetary spheres being accepted as the funda-mental structure of the cosmos. Famous observatories in Mus-lim countries include one established in Persia in 1074, in which one of the team members was the noted mathematician and sci-entist Omar Khayyam (through historical accident better known in Europe and America as a poet). Another notable observatory was established by Ulugh Beg in Samarqand (in modern-day Uzbekistan) in 1420, and it served as a model for early European observatories. The impact of the astronomy of the Muslims on Europe is indicated by the more than 200 stars whose names are derived from Arabic. Probably the last great example before colonial times was the series of observatories, which still may be visited today in Delhi and several other cities, constructed in northern India by the Hindu noble Jai Singh in the early 1700s; his observations, which he had compared with previous astro-nomical tables from Indian, Persian, and European sources, were presented to the Mughal emperor Muhammad Shah in 1728.

As with astronomy, there were religious motives for the fos-tering of medical science, in addition to the practical benefits for patrons who expected good medical attention. The creation of hospitals was a prominent philanthropic feature of precolo-nial Muslim societies. With the support of early rulers such as Caliph Harun al-Rashid in ninth-century Baghdad, leading physicians designed hospitals in major cities of the Near East, and notable examples may also be found in Muslim Spain, the Ottoman Empire, and Persia. Foundation documents for chari-table trusts supporting hospitals often not only specify the job descriptions and salaries of the medical and support staff, but they could also require that physicians meet every patient with a smile and avoid abusive language and attitudes.[26] One promi-nent example was the Mansuri hospital in Cairo, built in 1284.

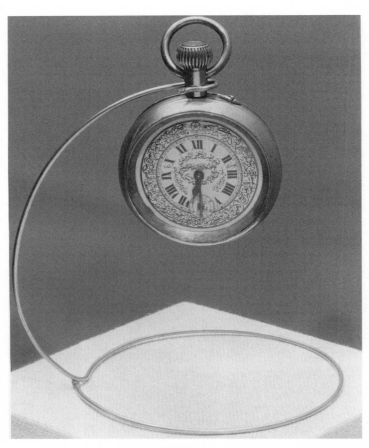

FIGURE 4.2

Pocketwatch made in Switzerland for a North Indian Muslim in the late nineteenth century, with an Urdu inscription and Arabic prayers and verses addressed to the five holy persons of Shi'ism. The compass in the stem helped to determine the direction of prayer toward Mecca. (The Ackland Art Museum, University of North Carolina at Chapel Hill, Ackland Fund, selected by The Ackland Associates)

This was an enormous facility based on a remodeled palace, with separate wards for men and women and a policy of open admission regardless of race, creed, or sex; all costs were borne by the hospital, and there was no limit to hospital stays. Leading physicians in Muslim countries built on the heritage of Greeks such as Hippocrates and Galen, and they added to it their own experience in terms of clinical practice and medicines. The great physician and philosopher Ibn Sina (known in Europe as Avicenna) became a standard authority not only in Persia and India but also in European universities, where his medical works were still taught in the 1600s.[27]

Although the achievements of medieval Muslim scientists have been duly recognized, they are almost always qualified as the product of a golden age now long gone. In histories of science and surveys of civilization it has become customary to speak of a decline taking place in Muslim countries, which led to their inevitable fall before the onslaughts of the superior European cultures. Although this attitude has become ingrained in most discussions of the subject, the chief spokesman for the "decline of Islam" theory in recent years has been former Princeton professor Bernard Lewis. In a series of writings over the past two decades, he has argued that Muslims became complacent about their political ascendancy during the late medieval period, so that they failed to take account of the changes in Europe in the early modern era. In particular, they lost any sense of curiosity about advances in the sciences and in technology, a fatal mistake that doomed them to defeat.[28] It is striking to see how similar this contention is to nineteenth-century colonial arguments about the disappearance of philosophy from Muslim countries. Indeed, for the anti-Semite scholar Ernst Renan, Arabs and Jews were equally incapable of either philosophy or science. The odd thing about this argument is that it requires no evidence. Since Muslims were allegedly incurious and unscientific, there is no need to look for intellectual production on their part in the postmedieval era.[29]

Recent research indicates, however, that there was a good deal more interchange between Muslims and European Christians in terms of science than has previously been imagined.[30] Although Europeans clearly developed superior technological applications of science with unprecedented success, particularly in fields such as naval and military technology, the efficient bureaucratic use of technology in the service of empire is quite different from basic scientific curiosity. In the seventeenth century, French physician François Bernier recorded his discussion of the scientific and philosophical theories of René Descartes and Pierre Gassendi with his employer, the talented Mughal minister Danishmand Khan, for whom he translated a number of relevant texts into Persian. Likewise, in the 1620s the Italian traveler Pietro della Valle translated the Latin astronomical works of Johannes Kepler into Persian for the benefit of Iranian intellectuals with whom he discussed many scientific and theological questions. One of the chief architects of the Taj Mahal wrote commentaries on the mathematical works of Euclid. Around 1654 the late Persian astronomer Muhammad Mahdi al-Yazdi produced two astrolabes containing maps of the northern and the southern celestial hemispheres, including new southern constellations recently discovered by Europeans. A number of Iranian and Indian Muslim travelers visited Europe in the eighteenth century, and several of them recorded their visits to European scientists and their discussions of scientific issues. Even as the South Indian Muslim ruler Tipu Sultan (d. 1799) sought help from the Ottomans and the French against an ultimately successful British invasion of his country, his minister Shushtari (a former employee of the East India Company) in 1801 recorded his reflections on the astronomical theories of Copernicus and Kepler. These are only a few of many examples of "homeless texts" that became irrelevant both to colonial regimes and to their nationalist successors.[31] In short, to say that Muslims after a certain point lacked intellectual curiosity and ignored science is simply wrong from a historical point of view. Like the similar thesis about the decline of philosophy in Muslim countries, the decline of science theory is based on selective amnesia. The presence and persistence of such misleading accounts of Muslim culture must once again be placed in the context of European colonialism and its justification.

It must be acknowledged, however, that by the end of the nineteenth century, European conquests had made good use not only of technology but also of the aura of scientific prestige. Despite the enormous destruction carried out by scientific means in the two world wars of the early twentieth century, science has become internationally the most respected discipline. In the great waves of immigration to Europe and America after decolonization, while Asian and African migrants to Europe were often laborers, many of those who went to North America aspired to the professions, preferably medicine, with engineering as an acceptable alternative. At the same time, the growth of modern universities in formerly colonized countries led to the creation of a significant educated class, particularly in engineering and sciences. Muslims who received scientific training had by no means relinquished their religious and cultural identity. They sought ways to integrate the truth of religion with the efficacy of science and technology. In this way arose a series of speculative theories connecting Islam and science.

In a way, the recent attempt to synthesize Islam and science resembles the reception of Greek philosophy and science by Muslims more than a thousand years earlier. In that case, however, Muslim intellectuals used philosophy as the main interpretive framework, and the Islamic religion was simply one example of how ethics and politics could be made accessible to the average person. Early Muslim philosophers differed from medieval Christian theologians, who considered philosophy to be the handmaid of Christian theology, simply a tool to assist in the comprehension of revelation. Instead, Muslim philosophers made the sheer intellectual discipline of philosophy into the benchmark against which religion must be measured, although they artfully disguised this strategy by announcing that revelation called for the study of philosophy.[32] The new effort to reconcile Islam and science in the twentieth century was not nearly as subtle. The assumption is that Islam is true and science is also true; therefore, Islam must in some sense include scientific truth. At the same time, there is a strongly anticolonial edge to this argument. Europeans maintained their superiority by claiming to be the exclusive representatives of science, and they cast Asia in the role of a backward and superstitious civilization that was enthralled by religious doctrine. To reverse this derogatory relationship, nineteenth-century Muslim thinkers initially claimed ownership over science, since they had given it to the Europeans.[33] This defensive argument had a flaw, however, in that it still involved accepting European dominance and buying into the notion of Islamic decline. The next step was taken by a number of Muslim authors who began to challenge exclusive European claims on science and modernity; this loose movement, which began after World War II, has been called "the Islamization of science."[34]

The most surprising entrant into this debate is a French physician who converted to Islam, Maurice Bucaille.[35] His basic thesis is that the Qur'an, unlike the Bible, has a remarkable amount of information that coincides with modern scientific discoveries in fields such as embryology; Bucaille's followers in Muslim countries have extended this thesis to include atomic physics. Since it is impossible for the Prophet Muhammad to have known this scientific material, it is therefore demonstrated that the Qur'an is inspired by divine revelation. In comparison, the Bible, with its many human editors, lacks this scientific depth and consequently cannot claim the same level of inspiration. Despite his eagerness to use scientific theories to interpret the Qur'an, Bucaille is clearly disturbed by the way that materialism has eroded the fabric of religious life. Like Christian fundamentalists, he finds Darwinian evolution to be disastrous for the religious concept of human nature as a divine creation. He therefore refers to evolution as a "theory," which cannot claim the factual status of either true science or true revelation.

The phenomenal success and popularity of Bucaille's theories is a remarkable testimony to the prestige that science enjoys today. Bucaille does not think of science as an experimental method that proceeds by falsifying hypotheses; instead, he regards it as a series of doctrines that, when proven, attain the status of fact. One problem with his identification of revelation and science is the changing nature of science itself, as several Muslim critics have observed.[36] How secure is the authority of religion if it is only being verified by the particular scientific theses that happen to be presently in effect? What should be said about the religious faith of millions of believers who accepted the Qur'an over the centuries, not because of modern science, but because of the charismatic power of the Prophet Muhammad and the message of the Qur'an itself? Although from this perspective the Islamization of science may appear to be a fallacy, it nevertheless has gained a considerable following among Muslims both in America and in Asia. The attraction of this theory is that it offers what rhetoricians call a totalizing theory, that is, an explanation that is monolithic and accounts for everything. It also provides an agenda for the Islamization of the social sciences, in order to provide an Islamic alternative to the value-free, supposedly objective framework of the secular university in fields such as anthropology, sociology, and economics.

In making such bold claims, the Islamization of science is a modern ideology that draws upon Islamic language and symbolism from an anticolonial perspective. Like "scientific creationists" who oppose Darwinian evolution from a Christian fundamentalist point of view, advocates of the Islamization of science consider it only fair to adopt the language and rhetoric of science in order to challenge the hegemony of atheism and materialism in public life today. In sociological terms, it is striking to see that this discourse on Islam and science has emerged primarily among contemporary Muslims who have been initially trained as scientists and engineers, not among the traditional religious scholars. It is, interestingly, from the same science and engineering groups in Muslim countries that fundamentalist movements draw many of their supporters. This mechanistic and rationalistic approach to religious texts has proved appealing to a significant proportion of contemporary Muslims. Critics charge that this confusion of science and religion distorts both subjects.

The dilemma over the relationship between science and religion is certainly not unique to Muslims. The so-called warfare between science and religion that has episodically occurred in Europe and America has formed an important chapter in the modern history of Christianity, from the trial of Galileo to the Scopes "monkey trial" of 1920. Skirmishes are still taking place in American schools over control of the biology curriculum and the question of equal time for the doctrine of creation. Just as it is unlikely that Christian fundamentalists will give up on their resistance to secularism in the schools, in the same way an ideological placement of Islam in relation to science still proves an attractive option to some Muslims. Indeed, both in Muslim majority countries and among immigrant Muslim minorities, the Islamization of science may continue to enjoy political protection for some time to come.

Despite the efforts of some theologians and scientists to reach creative solutions about the relationship between nature and God, many, regardless of their religion, see science (or at least its technological applications) as an authoritative system of social control. New discoveries, particularly in the life sciences and medicine, are raising troubling ethical issues for which no religious tradition has ready answers. Muslims, like members of other religions, will need to look deeply into the resources of their predecessors to find principles that they can apply in these new situations.

CHAPTER 5

SPIRITUALITY IN PRACTICE

Early Sufism and the
Cultivation of Mystical Experience

Spirituality is often contrasted with religion as being more personal, less authoritative, and definitely more interesting. This disenchantment with institutional religion is a recent development in European and American societies, although it has also affected other cultures. The concept of religious experience, which was memorably explored more than a century ago by psychologist William James, reflects a distinctively Protestant and even American view of religion.[1] Experience, which is related to the notion of experiment, was a radical concept at the time of the Protestant Reformation; it suggested the rejection of the dogmatic orthodoxy of the Catholic Church, and the individual search for authenticity. Another radical context for the notion of experience was alchemy, a scientific and religious enterprise in which mavericks and seekers used experimentation to contest the orthodoxy of Aristotelian doctrines about nature.[2] Perusing the best-seller lists in the category of spirituality, one must go through dozens of titles before reaching those that are concerned with formal and institutional religion; frequently, bookstores interfile books on spirituality in the large section on health and self-help, while religion is left to a small and forlorn stack of Bibles and other authoritative texts. College professors wryly acknowledge that students consider a course called "Medieval Judaism" to be boring and unattractive, but if it is repackaged as "Jewish Spirituality," there may be a waiting list to get into the class.

Parallel to spirituality is mysticism, and both concepts have taken on an aura of magic and mystery that has displaced the original meaning of both terms. Spirituality originally signified nonmaterial concerns, but it also overlapped with the ecclesiastical institutions of the church. It is sometimes confused with spiritualism, the occult practice of summoning the spirits of the recently departed, which was so popular in nineteenth-century America. Likewise, mysticism refers to what is called a negative theology, because it describes God as "not this, not that," as a being whose ultimate reality is beyond rational conception; the classic formulation is found in the *Mystical Theology* of Dionysius, written by a fourth-century Eastern Christian author who was steeped in Neoplatonic philosophy.[3] By extension, mysticism refers to experiences of union with God, or the ultimate reality, however it is conceived. Probably because mysticism deals with what lies beyond rationality, it is often described as obscure and muddled thinking, and popular culture identifies mysticism with magic and occult powers. When I have asked students to identify a typical mystic, the most frequently suggested name is Nostradamus (d. 1566), the obscure French prophet whose enigmatic quatrains have been used to predict any manner of events. Much better examples of both spirituality and mysticism would be St. John of the Cross, St. Teresa of Avila, or Meister Eckhart, all of whom are regarded as mystics by the Catholic Church. None of them bothered with predicting the future or with producing miracles (although the Catholic Church has verified the status of the two saints by their posthumous miracles as witnessed by others). Instead, these mystics recorded intense spiritual meditations and experiences in prose and poetry of extraordinary quality. Contrary to the modern notion of independent spirituality, most medieval Christian mystics belonged to highly organized and disciplined monastic orders that were firmly under the hierarchical authority of the church. So when attempting to apply the concept of mysticism in an Islamic context, we need to recognize the limitations of the term, whether in historical usage or in the current popular perception.

It is often said that the mystical aspect of Islam is Sufism.[4] One often encounters Sufism today in the freewheeling market of spirituality and New Age self-expression, but like Christian spirituality and mysticism, it has an institutional history also. The term Sufi comes from the Arabic word for wool (*suf*), which was the rough garment of ascetics and prophets in the Near East, symbolizing self-denial. Currently, the best-known representative of Sufism is the classical Persian poet Rumi, who is often represented as someone who transcended all religions.[5] Many people wonder what relationship, if any, Sufism has to Islam. This debate is not new; from the time European scholars began to conceptualize these subjects two centuries ago, they viewed Sufism as an attractive form of universal spirituality. In their view, Sufism (an English word with the characteristic "-ism" ending of modern ideologies) could have nothing to do with what they considered the dry and legalistic religion of Islam. Although European scholars assumed that Sufism therefore had to derive from Indian yoga or some other extra-Islamic source, Sufi spiritual circles used a religious vocabulary based almost entirely on Arabic and Islamicate sources. The European concepts of Sufism and Islam were in effect separated at birth, when they were naturalized in English and other languages early in the nineteenth century. Modern Muslim reformists subsequently mirrored the Europeans in regarding Sufism as something apart from Islam; the difference lay in the reformists' negative evaluation of Sufism as an innovation and a foreign intrusion into Islam, while the Orientalists saw Sufism as something positive. Yet this negative attitude of reformist Muslims toward Sufism is relatively recent; for most of Islamic history, this form of spirituality and mystical practice has been a major feature of Muslim societies.[6]

Historically speaking, Muslim spiritual life begins with the Qur'an and the Prophet Muhammad, which are inextricably linked. As an example, one may cite the famous Qur'anic passage on "the Night of Power," commonly regarded as the night on which the revelation of the Qur'an was delivered to the Prophet: "Truly we caused it to descend on the Night of Power. And what shall inform you of the Night of Power? The Night of Power is better than a thousand months. On it descended the angels, and the Spirit, with the permission of their Lord, with every command. It is peace, until the break of day" (97:1–5). The act of revelation is shown as the descent of the spirit, which elicits a corresponding movement in the ascension of the Prophet through the heavens to meet God. This dialectic of divine presence and prophetic ascent became the model of spiritual experience for later generations of Muslims. Muhammad in particular is the exemplar of spirituality for Sufis, who strive to imitate him both in his external religious practice and in his inner spiritual states. His saying, "I came only for the perfection of character," is an indication of his role as a guide. Sufis came to view Muhammad as the being of light whose creation preceded the creation of the universe. His mission was universal, and in his compassion he alone of all the prophets would intercede on behalf of all humanity.

Joined to the basis of mystical experience was the notion of spiritual community, which the Sufis trace back to the "People of the Bench," a group of Muslims in the early Medina community whose only home was a portico in the mosque. They stand as the first example of organized spiritual life based on a community that shared everything. The earliest Sufi circles formed around individuals of intense piety who brought an ascetic impulse to their meditation on the Qur'an. This turn away from worldly enticements was significant at a time when the early Arab empire enjoyed an unparalleled concentration of wealth and power. Early figures such as al-Hasan al-Basri (d. 728) had a major effect on their contemporaries through public preaching and through their writings, and they drew attention to the need for psychological introspection and moral analysis as part of obedience to the commands of God. These leaders formed relations with followers and associates that were informal and highly personal, but they were initially known as ascetics and devotees; the term "Sufi" did not come into general use until about 800 C.E.

The Spirituality of Shi'ism

Sufism was by no means the only form of spirituality among Muslims. Philosophy, though pursued by a relatively small number of specialists, was an important resource for reflection on theology and prophecy. The mystical tendencies of Greek philosophers like Plotinus found their echo in the meditations and speculations of Muslim philosophers such as Ibn Sina, Suhrawardi, and Mulla Sadra. A much more extensive form of Muslim spirituality developed in the various Shi'i movements that proliferated during the early Islamic centuries. Shi'ism takes its name from the party or faction (*shi'a* in Arabic) that saw 'Ali (the cousin and son-in-law of Muhammad) as the legitimate successor to the Prophet.[7] Although the dispute over succession to the Prophet had an obvious political character, the debate over the qualifications for this office led to speculation about the spiritual basis of authority and charisma. The supporters of 'Ali reflected a widely held discontent when they objected to the nepotistic policies of the third caliph, 'Uthman, whom they accused of treating the imperial treasury as a personal bank account. What distinguished the committed followers of 'Ali was their conviction that Muhammad had deliberately bequeathed his authority and his spiritual knowledge directly to 'Ali, thus designating him as his only lawful successor. The occasion on which Muhammad declared 'Ali his successor, at a place called Ghadir Khumm, is celebrated by Shi'is as an annual event of great importance. 'Ali eventually gained recognition as the fourth caliph, although the Umayyad family (from the old Meccan aristocracy) opposed him, and after 'Ali's assassination the Umayyads turned the caliphate into a royal dynasty. These unfortunate events convinced many of 'Ali's followers that the forces of injustice were inevitably opposed to the true holders of spiritual authority.

The later development of Shi'ism turned upon the radical opposition between the rightful religious leader (*imam*) of the community and the de facto ruling caliph, who was only the military commander (*amir*) of the empire. Those Muslims who accepted the political status quo, regardless of the justice of the case, eventually became known as Sunni—meaning that they considered themselves followers of the example of the Prophet (*sunna*). For the Sunni Muslims, *imam* (literally meaning "in front") is simply a generic term for the leader of community prayer, but for the Shi'is, the Imam is the supreme representative of divine authority on earth (capitalizing this term is a good way of signaling the unique Shi'i emphasis on the office of the Imam). Since 'Ali was regarded as the first Imam, his sons, Hasan and Husayn (both grandsons of the Prophet), were obviously his successors. Although Hasan did not take any public stand against the Umayyad ruler, Husayn led an unsuccessful revolt with a small band of followers, who were all killed in battle in 680 C.E. The Imams descended from these early leaders were renowned for their piety, and many of them spent their lives in virtual imprisonment under the watchful eye of the caliphs.

There are several major divisions among the Shi'is who revere the Imams as the rightful successors of the Prophet; they have diverged mostly over questions of succession to the office of the Imam. The largest group is the Twelver Shi'is, who believe in twelve Imams beginning with 'Ali; the last of these Imams disappeared late in the ninth century, and he is expected to return as the Messiah at Judgment Day. Approximately 10 to 15 percent of Muslims today (around 150 million people) are Twelver Shi'is; they predominate in Iran and Iraq and form significant minorities in Pakistan, Lebanon, and other countries. Another notable branch of Shi'ism is the Isma'ilis, whose present Imam is the Agha Khan, the forty-ninth hereditary successor to the Prophet in this lineage.[8] About 15 million in number (comparable to the world Jewish population), the Isma'ilis are found principally in Pakistan, India, East Africa, and Tajikistan, with significant communities in the Middle East, Europe, and North America. A smaller group is the Dawoodi Bohras, a community of perhaps 1 million people centered in Western India. Their current leader, Syedna Mohammed Burhanuddin, is the fifty-second successor to the Prophet in this tradition.[9] Other offshoots of Shi'ism include the Nusayris, otherwise known as Alevis in Turkey or 'Alawis in Syria, and the Druze of Lebanon and Israel.

Central to the vision of Shi'ism is the notion of the Imam as the charismatic leader who is endowed with supreme wisdom and authority. As remarked previously, it is a fundamental assumption in Shi'ism that God will not deny the grace of divine guidance to humanity. Although Shi'is accept the finality of the prophethood of Muhammad, the ongoing fact of guidance is both a logical and an existential necessity. Shi'i Muslims look to the early Imams for direction and aid, and their sayings form a supplementary body of hadith that has scriptural authority second only to the hadith of the Prophet. The prayers, writings, and speeches of 'Ali, collected in the tenth century under the title *The Peak of Eloquence*, are a particularly important resource.[10] Although there were major doctrinal debates over the exact status of the Imams, they clearly fulfilled the very necessary role of ongoing interpreters of God's will. Shi'is focus particular reverence on five holy persons, "the people of the [Prophet's] household" (*ahl al-bayt*): Muhammad, his daughter Fatima, 'Ali, Hasan, and Husayn (although the "hand of Fatima" symbolizes these five holy persons among Shi'is, it is widely found as a decorative symbol in Sunni contexts as well). When Fatima and Muhammad are included with the twelve Imams, this group is collectively known as the Fourteen Immaculates, since God has preserved them from sin. Shi'is regard Fatima with special reverence; she is said to have been created, like the Imams, from a primordial light, and her life was filled with miraculous events. Scholars have compared her role in Shi'ism to the position of the Virgin Mary for Roman Catholics.[11] Some followers of the Imams, usually called extremists, adored them with such excessive reverence that they practically treated them as God. Although most Shi'is rejected outright deification of their leaders, they nevertheless regarded the Imams as beings endowed with supernatural knowledge and virtue.[12]

The Twelver Shi'is in particular have focused on the persecution of the Imams, who according to their belief were murdered by their opponents (except the Twelfth Imam, whose advent is awaited). This tragic view of history has led to the creation of rituals of lamentation, in which the faithful acknowledge the terrible sufferings of the most virtuous of all humanity. The sufferings of the Imams are not in vain, however; they are an unavoidable sacrifice that ultimately works for the redemption of humanity. Shi'is mark the anniversary of the martyrdom of Husayn with poems and stories of mourning and lamentation every year on the tenth of the month of Muharram. Some worshipers even perform severe physical penance in sympathy with

the sufferings of the Imams.[13] In Iran the stories of the martyr-
doms of the Imams have developed into elaborate dramatic cycles of passion plays performed by amateur actors.[14] All this will
remind some readers of Christian teachings of atonement and
the redemption of humanity by the sufferings of Jesus. There is
certainly some similarity between these teachings, although the
Shi'i Muslim focus on the Imams is clearly independent of the
Christian attitude toward Jesus.

The Imams and other members of the Prophet's family function as intermediaries between the ordinary believer and God.
In Twelver Shi'ism, the physical absence of the Imam means that
members of the current religious hierarchy act in his place as his
representatives. The role of Shi'i religious scholars has been
consequently much weightier than that of their Sunni counterparts.[15] Not only do Shi'i religious scholars claim independent
authority to make judgments in law, they also have incidentally
ruled that alms taxes should be paid directly to them, rather
than through existing governments. This policy was responsible
for the extensive landholdings of the Iranian religious hierarchy,
which the last shah of Iran attempted to seize through policies
of land reform. In any case, the tombs of the Imams and their
family members have become important places of pilgrimage.
The holy sites in Iraq containing the shrines of 'Ali, Husayn,
and other Imams are particularly important pilgrimage sites
for all Shi'is.[16] In Iran the two most important shrines are in
Mashhad (the tomb of the eighth Imam, 'Ali Reza) and in Qom
(the mausoleum of Fatima bint Musa, daughter of the seventh
Imam).

The logic of spiritual mediation calls for some comment because of the tremendous success of Protestantism in leveling the
notion of spiritual hierarchies and elites. While Catholic and
Orthodox Christians still accept the idea that God can single out
saints and endow them with extraordinary holiness and grace,

Protestants prefer a more democratic approach to religion. In this view, all human beings have equal access to God, and no one is in the privileged position. The concept of sainthood demands a different understanding, however. If it is possible for some people to be much closer to God than others, they are, as it were, spiritual athletes, who through a combination of their own effort and divine grace have obtained extraordinary status. To use an older political model, access to God is more like a traditional monarchy; despite theoretical equal access, there are gatekeepers who must be approached to get into the inner sanctum. The Imams and saints have greater practical access to the divine court, and therefore they can be of enormous assistance to ordinary believers. The strength of the personal relationships that many Muslims feel with the Imams and saints is certainly remarkable, as any visitor can see by the emotional behavior of pilgrims at their shrines.

Just as Protestant reformers found it necessary to destroy the Catholic monasteries and shrines of England, the puritanical movement of the Wahhabis undertook a similar campaign against the tombs of Shi'i Imams and Sufi saints. When religious reformer Ibn 'Abd al-Wahhab (founder of the Wahhabi movement) allied himself with the Saudi family late in the eighteenth century, the new ideology became a potent force unifying the tribal coalition. In 1801 Wahhabi forces raiding Iraq destroyed the dome of the tomb of Imam Husayn in Kerbela. More than a century later, when the Saudi family consolidated the hold of its monarchy over Arabia, they carried out a massive demolition of all the tombs in Medina, particularly the tombs of Imams and members of the family of Muhammad.[17] According to some accounts, there was even a proposal to raze the tomb of the Prophet Muhammad in order to prevent idolatrous worship of him, but the structure was preserved as part of the original mosque of Medina. The anniversary of this destruction of the

"Eternal Paradise" cemetery in 1925 is still marked by Shi'is with great sadness.

The disagreement between Wahhabis and Shi'is over intercession and mediation is serious. Wahhabis consider that any excessive reverence directed at a human being is simply a form of polytheism and idolatry and a rejection of true monotheism. Therefore their authorities have declared that undertaking a pilgrimage to Mecca with the intention of also visiting the tomb of the Prophet in Medina negates the value of the pilgrimage. As recently as 1990 a senior Saudi religious official, Shaykh Bin Jibrin, declared that Shi'is deserve to be killed, and repression of the significant Shi'i minority in Arabia continues to be a problem. It is likely that the motives of the Wahhabis in combating pilgrimage to shrines were more than theological. The shrines of both Shi'i Imams and Sufi saints were centers of tremendous wealth and power, often connected to income derived from land taxation as well as pious donations. The Wahhabis certainly appreciated the way in which the shrines institutionalized certain kinds of entrenched religious authority, which they often criticized as being corrupt in any case. The eradication of tomb-shrines was a powerful symbol of the extension of their religious authority over all Muslims, particularly when this was carried out in the central holy places of Arabia.

Later Sufism

The outstanding Sufi leaders of the ninth and tenth centuries, such as Abu Yazid al-Bistami, Junayd al-Baghdadi (d. 910), and others, later became known retrospectively as the central organizers of the Sufi movement. The growth of this movement led to the development of a biographical and historical account of

Sufism in which early ascetics and pious leaders were viewed as a chain of masters and disciples who had safeguarded and transmitted a mystical knowledge that had originated with the Prophet. The early theorists of Sufism had described it as parallel to the standard Islamic religious sciences, to which it added the internal knowledge of divine realities. By the fourteenth century, leading scholars such as Ibn Khaldun acknowledged Sufism as an integral part of religious knowledge. The spiritual practices of this movement were not, however, carried out by isolated individuals in a spontaneous and unconnected fashion. There was a gradual accumulation of shared knowledge and practice over centuries by large numbers of people who committed themselves to intensifying and internalizing their relationship with God and the Prophet. It is this collective historical tradition that we describe by the name of Sufism.

One important institutional feature of Sufism was the tomb of the Sufi saint, which increasingly became a focus of local pilgrimage. The Sufi manuals had clarified the status of the "friend of God," or saint, as one who is perfect in obedience to God and who is sustained by the love of God. The Sufi concept of sainthood clearly took as its model the sanctity of the Imams in Shi'ism. The saints were seen as the invisible supports of the world, a hierarchy of holy men and women who were under God's protection. While it may have been rare to obtain the direct guidance of Sufi saints during their lifetime, nothing prevented people of all classes from seeking the aid of the saints after their demise; saints, it must be recalled, like martyrs, were not regarded as really dead but were still living and conscious in the grave. In this way saints became intercessors for those who approached them, both for everyday needs and at the Day of Judgment.

The tombs of many Sufi saints were typically erected at or near their homes. Under Islamic law the ownership and maintenance of these tombs fell to family members and descendants, who may or may not have had spiritual aspirations. In later generations the devotion of many pilgrims thus supported a class of hereditary custodians who were in charge of the finances and operations of the tomb-shrines, which could be combined with a functioning hospice where Sufi teaching took place or with other institutions such as mosques, open kitchens, or religious academies. Increasingly, however, the Sufi tomb came to be an independent institution, in some cases functioning as the center of a massive pilgrimage at the annual festival of the saint. These festivals were variously described as the saint's birthday (*mawlid*) in the Mediterranean region or "wedding" (*'urs*) in Iran and India; the latter case symbolically celebrated the death anniversary as the "wedding" of the saint's soul with God. The tombs of especially popular saints eventually were surrounded with royal burial grounds where kings and members of the nobility would erect their own tombs to acquire a borrowed holiness or to benefit in the afterlife from the pious exercises of pilgrims to the nearby saints. Examples of this kind of necropolis include the Sufi shrines of Khuldabad and Gulbarga in the Indian Deccan, Tatta in Pakistan, and the various graveyards of Cairo.

In many cases Sufi tombs and hospices became cultural centers as well, where distinctive kinds of music and poetry were often heard. Thus the Arabic poetry of the noted Sufi poet Ibn al-Farid (d. 1235) in Cairo has been regularly recited at his tomb before mass audiences, particularly at his annual festival.[18] Likewise, Indian Chishti shrines continue to be centers for recitation of poetry in musical sessions known as *qawwali*. At major festivals in South Asia, such as the anniversary of the death of Baba Farid in Pakistan, one can hear dozens of singers compete for the honor of singing before the saint's tomb, mixing lyrics in Persian with verses in Hindi, Punjabi, Sindhi, and other Indian languages.[19] Special local traditions of music developed in Turkish hospices and shrines with poetry of a style quite different from court poetry, and performance styles at musical sessions included the measured dance of the Mevlevi Sufis, or "whirling dervishes."[20] In North Africa other distinctive musical styles developed in the Sufi shrines using Greek physiological theories of the four humors to effect healing based on bodily sympathies of particular musical modes.[21] In West Africa the Senegalese Sufi order of the Mouridiyya has developed a strong tradition of devotional music praising the Sufi saints, and this music has affected popular music through internationally known performers like Youssou N'Dour; the Mourides also employ the visual arts to engage their devotees.[22]

The most decisive institutional formation of Sufism was the establishment of Sufi orders. While it is convenient to refer to these organizations as orders, with an implicit analogy to the monastic orders of medieval Christianity (Franciscans, Dominicans, etc.), it is not an exact analogy. Sufi orders are much less centrally organized than their Christian counterparts, they do not as a rule observe celibacy, and they have a more fluid hierarchical structure. These orders originated in a less formal fashion as well. A number of outstanding personalities of the twelfth and thirteenth centuries lent their names to associations that developed individual spiritual methods or "ways" (*tariqas*), including special formulations of the names of God for meditative repetition (*dhikr*). Each of these associations became known as a way or as a chain (*silsila*), with masters and disciples constituting the links. These chains were traced backward in time, ending with the Prophet Muhammad. Nearly all of these chains reached Muhammad via his son-in-law and cousin 'Ali; frequently there are parallel chains including the early Shi'i Imams, who are commonly revered in Sufi circles, even though the majority of Sufi orders have a Sunni orientation (there are also several Shi'i Sufi orders, particularly in Iran). An interesting variation occurs with the Naqshbandi order, which reaches the Prophet through Abu Bakr as his first successor, preserving an anti-Shi'i tonality that is unusual in Sufism (nevertheless, the Naqshbandis include the eighth Imam in their lineage). Complicating the concept of the Sufi order is the phenomenon of multiple initiation, observable since the fifteenth century, through which individual Sufis could receive instruction in the methods of several different orders while maintaining a primary allegiance to one.

The major impact of the Sufi orders in terms of religion was the popularization of the spiritual practices of the Sufis on a mass scale. The interior orientation of the informal movement of early Sufism became available to a much wider public through participation in shrine rituals, the circulation of accounts of holy lives, and the publicizing of various degrees of instruction through recitation of the names of God. Elaborate initiation rituals took place in which the master's presentation of articles such as a dervish cloak, hat, or staff would signify the disciple's entrance into the order. A common feature of initiation was the requirement that the disciple copy by hand the genealogical "tree" of the order, linking the disciple to the entire chain of masters going back to the Prophet.

Some of the Sufi orders, such as the Qadiriyya (named after 'Abd al-Qadir Jilani, d. 1166), are spread throughout Islamic lands from North Africa to Southeast Asia. Others are more regional in scope, like the Shadhiliyya in North Africa (named after Abu al-Hasan al-Shadhili, d. 1258) or the Chishtiyya in India and Pakistan (named after Mu'in al-Din Chishti, d. 1236). Particular orders are known for distinctive practices, such as the loud *dhikr* recitation of the Rifa'iyya, in contrast to the silent *dhikr* favored by the Naqshbandiyya. Some orders, including the Chishtiyya and the Mevleviyya, have integrated music and even dance into their practice, while other orders resolutely shun these activities as distractions to spiritual training. Sometimes Sufi leaders, such as the early Chishti masters, tried to keep political power at arm's length, and they advised their followers to refuse offers of land endowment. Certain Sufi masters demonstrated their disdain of the world by refusing to entertain rulers or visit them at court.

On the other hand, certain orders have a history of close association with political power; the Suhrawardiyya and the Naqshbandiyya in India and Iran felt it was important to influence rulers in the proper religious direction, and the Bektashiyya had strong links to the elite Ottoman troops known as the Janissaries. The Safawiyya, once a moderate Sunni order based at Ardebil, became widespread among Turkish tribes on the Persian-Ottoman frontier, and it emerged with a strongly Shi'i and messianic character to become the basis for the Safavid Empire that ruled Iran from the sixteenth through the eighteenth centuries. During the period of nineteenth-century colonialism, when much of the Islamic world fell under European domination, Sufi institutions played varied roles. Hereditary custodians of Sufi shrines in places such as the Indian Punjab were treated as important local landlords by colonial officials, and they became further entrenched as political leaders due to British patronage; ironically, the cooperation of these Sufi leaders became essential in later independence movements directed against British control. Similarly, the Senegalese order known as the Mouridiyya became heavily involved in peanut farming, with the support of French colonial authorities, and they have emerged in the postcolonial order as a major social institution. With the overthrow of traditional elites by European conquest, Sufi orders in some regions remained the only surviving Islamic social structures, and they furnished the principal leadership for anticolonial struggles in places such as Algeria, Libya, the Caucasus, and China. French administrators in North Africa, therefore, viewed Sufi orders with suspicion, and colonial scholars produced police dossiers on the Sufi orders, designed to predict their possible reactions to official policies.

In the postcolonial period, Sufi orders and institutions have an ambiguous position. Governments in many Muslim countries have inherited the centralized bureaucratic organization of their colonial predecessors, and countries like Egypt and Pakistan have attempted to subject the orders and shrines to government control. Officials frequently appear at Sufi festivals and attempt to connect popular reverence for saints with support for the regime. Nonetheless, many of the most significant Sufi organizations flourish without official recognition. Contemporary fundamentalist movements attack Sufism with a virulence only slightly less intense than that reserved for anti-Western diatribes. Pilgrimage to Sufi tombs is frequently denounced as an idolatry that treats humans on the level of God. Modernists and secularists also criticize Sufism for many of the same activities, but in their minds the problem is medieval superstition and the manipulation of the credulous masses. Sufi orders have been illegal in Turkey since the 1920s, when Kemal Ataturk secularized the Turkish state. The performance of the Sufi rituals such as the "whirling dervish" dance of the Mevlevis is tolerated only as a cultural activity and is exported abroad through touring companies and sound recordings; the tomb of the great Sufi poet Jalal al-Din Rumi, which many visitors treat as a shrine, is officially listed as a museum. Sufi activities are not publicly tolerated in countries such as Saudi Arabia and Iran, since Sufi leaders and tomb cults would constitute an unacceptable alternative spiritual authority. Still, it is remarkable that the founders of certain fundamentalist movements, such as the Muslim Brotherhood in Egypt and the Jama'at-i Islami in India, were exposed to Sufi orders in their youth, and they seem to have adapted certain organizational techniques and leadership styles from Sufism; the main difference is that these movements substitute ideology for Sufi spirituality in order to become mass political parties in the modern nation-state.

In recent years Sufi orders have extended their reach into Europe and the Americas, and today there are branches of orders from India, Iran, North Africa, and Turkey active in major urban centers in many Western countries. Some groups derived from Sufi orders have only tenuous associations with Islam, and they present Sufism as a mystical universal religion that may be pursued through dancing and chanting, without requiring the practice of ritual prayer or other duties of Islamic law. Other groups have more emphatic relations with Islam, even including insistence on the clothing and customs of the order's country of origin. While it is too soon to predict the future of Sufism in the West, it seems certain to take on some aspects of modern American and European culture, such as joint participation of men and women in contexts where gender separation was the norm in many premodern Muslim societies. At the same time, Sufism in the West strives to preserve many of the distinctive rituals and institutions of traditional Sufism, such as tombs of Sufi masters who have died in America, which have now become pilgrimage sites. In any case, Sufi orders are surviving despite the restrictions of modern governments and the opposition of fundamentalists, and they continue to act as channels that both preserve the influence of saints of the past and make possible a more direct personal access to God and the Prophet through spiritual discipline.

The tight organizational structure of Sufi orders with masters and disciples, together with networks of tomb-shrines, is not the only way Sufism is being felt today. The poetry of Rumi has become a best-selling publishing phenomenon through translator-poets such as Coleman Barks and Robert Bly. Other major Sufis like Ibn 'Arabi are becoming increasingly known in translation to a range of Muslim and non-Muslim readers. The cultural products of Sufism, especially in the form of music, have generated an international following in the category of world music through outstanding performers such as the late Nusrat Fateh Ali Khan.[23] While some may find institutional Sufism to be authoritarian, the charting of the inner range of spiritual experience in Sufism offers a resource that has a wide appeal today.

What Is Islamic Art?

The expression of spirituality and religion in relation to culture is often sought in the form of art and creativity. Certainly the history of Christian spirituality cannot be divorced from its expression in painting, architecture, and other arts. So in the same way, we expect a comparable category of Islamic art to have a corresponding role in relation to Islamic spirituality.[24] The aesthetic dimension undoubtedly has a profound significance for Muslim cultures, and it springs naturally from the celebration of divine creativity. As the Prophet observed in a celebrated hadith, "God is beautiful and loves beauty." Although the subject of Islamic art could cover music and literature as well as architecture, for simplicity I will restrict this discussion to visual art and objects that might be seen in museums. Yet on closer examination, even this restricted concept of Islamic art is surprisingly hard to define. As two prominent art historians have pointed out, "It is easier to say what Islamic art is not than what it is. . . . Islamic art refers neither to art of a specific era nor to that of a particular place or people. . . . Islamic art is neither a style nor a movement, and the people who made it were not necessarily

Muslims. . . . Whereas some Islamic art was undoubtedly made by Christians and Jews for Muslim patrons, some 'Islamic' art made by Muslims was intended for Christians or Jews."[25] Considering the question of Islamic art raises a number of related issues: the nature of religious art in general, the identity of users and patrons as well as makers of art, the representation of Muslims in European art, and Muslim participation in modern art.

The category of Islamic art was, in reality, coined by non-Muslim scholars to describe beautiful artifacts coming from Muslim countries.[26] There is no equivalent term in premodern Islamic cultures, although in modern times the European phrase "fine arts" has been translated directly into Arabic and other languages. From an early date, artisans in different Muslim countries produced objects of high quality both for daily use and for the luxury market; at various times, particularly after the seventeenth century, Europeans were greatly interested in collecting and even imitating high-quality artifacts from Muslim regions. To a great extent, this artistic production simply continued the traditions of existing arts from those regions (Syria, Persia, India, Egypt, etc.). There was not necessarily anything about them that directly related to the Islamic faith, although pottery and metalwork, for instance, gradually came to include wise sayings and advice written in Arabic, which might have some more or less religious content. In the same way, monuments of Islamic architecture used forms that were already current throughout the ancient world (the dome, the octagon, pillared galleries, etc.). With the possible exception of the sculpted stalactite form called *muqarnas* (the delicate geometrical tracery found in transition zones from domes to walls), there is hardly a single architectural element that could be considered uniquely Islamic.[27]

In Europe for the past 200 years the term "art" has meant fine arts that are not for use, in contrast to crafts produced for everyday needs. Yet in major collections of Islamic art in the museums of New York or Washington, D.C., alongside miniature paintings one can find a huge variety of beautiful but mundane objects, ranging from pencil cases to candlesticks, inkwells, metalwork, book bindings, carpets, coins, swords, and jewelry. As in so many other cases, in art, too, there has been a tendency to consider all the products of Muslim societies as the results of religion, although we probably would not refer to ordinary crafts produced in medieval Europe as "Christian art." It only makes sense to call art Islamic if it is directly connected to religion; the larger cultural sphere that is connected to Islamic religion can be called Islamicate, keeping in mind that Islamicate culture includes nonreligious activities and participation of non-Muslims.

Another way to understand the problem of Islamic art is to distinguish between religious art, defined as art with religious themes, and sacred art, which is art used in ritual for sacred purposes.[28] Islamic religious art would thus include books with miniature illustrations containing stories about prophets and saints. Islamic sacred art would comprise finely calligraphed Qur'ans and prayer books, ornate mosque lamps, prayer carpets, and the architecture of the mosque itself—in short, art that is used for religious practice. Paintings with religious content relating to Islam are not empty of religious significance, but since they have no function in religious practice, they could not be considered sacred. All the other everyday items produced by artisans in majority Muslim countries are best called Islamicate, both because they lack direct religious significance and because they can be produced and consumed by Muslims as well as non-Muslims.

The mention of miniature paintings raises the well-known issue of the prohibition of images in Islamic law. Many people have the impression that Islamic law decrees an absolute ban on portraits of living creatures, on the grounds that images and representations of human beings encourage idolatry and attempt to usurp divine creativity. The history of Islamic art demonstrates, however, that pictorial art has a long and vigorous tradition. The status of images in Islamic law is quite complex. The Qur'an itself makes no direct reference to painting and the visual arts, though like the Hebrew Bible it firmly rejects the idolatrous worship of anything other than God. There are several hadith reported where Muhammad apparently condemned specific objects with images of humans or animals, but it is debated whether the condemnation extended to all images or merely to the context in which they were found (in one case, Muhammad was distracted from prayer by curtains embroidered with figures, but he had no objection to them being trimmed and used as pillow cases).

In any case, Muslims frequently employed images in secular contexts, including mural paintings in royal palaces and book illustrations of subjects ranging from botany and astronomy to tales of the prophets. In general, however, it is true that images have generally been rejected in Muslim sacred places. Important exceptions include the Umayyad mosque of Damascus, erected early in the eighth century, with mosaic depictions of a heavenly landscape of rivers, trees, and buildings, but it is noteworthy that it contains no human or animal figures. The absence of images in Islamic sacred art has a parallel in the iconoclastic movement of Eastern Christianity, which saw a large-scale rejection of image worship at roughly the same time as the beginning phase of Islamic civilization (eighth to ninth centuries). On the other hand, the proliferation of images through modern technology and styles of mass political art derived from socialist countries have yielded surprising changes in some localities. The new mausoleum of Ayatollah Khomeini in Tehran, like many sacred Shi'i shrines in that country, contains gigantic free-standing portraits of Khomeini and his martyred son Ahmad, reminiscent of the massive paintings of Lenin or Chairman Mao that were displayed in Russia and China not long ago. Cemeteries devoted to martyrs of the Iranian revolution or the Iran-Iraq war are filled with photographs of the departed. Similarly, in Iran one constantly sees popular portraits of Muhammad, 'Ali, and Husayn, either as full-sized posters or in the form of postcards available in any shop (see fig. 5.1). While Muslims in other countries might find this objectionable, it seems to cause no comment in Iran.

The artistic creativity of Muslims turned to new nonfigural forms that have become easily recognized and distinctive hallmarks of Islamic art. The chief nonfigural elements of Islamic art, whether in small decorated objects or major monuments, are calligraphy, vegetal ornamentation, and geometric pattern. The infinitely repeating patterns of vegetal ornamentation and geometry, often called arabesque, fill the margins of books and the walls of buildings with a constant reminder of the beauty and order that is the basis of the universe.[29] Calligraphy derives its prestige from the sacred book of the Qur'an. Although the Arabic script existed in pre-Islamic times, it became a highly developed art form over a period of centuries in both sacred and secular contexts. As the vehicle for the word of God, the Arabic script was employed in Qur'ans to permit the contemplation of the divine beauty, and this formed the basis for a calligraphic aesthetic in multiple styles that extended to all languages that used the Arabic script (including Persian, Turkish, and Urdu).[30]

The particular messages conveyed by the texts spelled out in Arabic script were also crucial to the meaning of the buildings they adorned. The Dome of the Rock in Jerusalem quotes verses from the Qur'an on the Islamic doctrine of the human nature of Jesus; the monument thus stands as an imperial statement against the Christian ideology of the rival Byzantine Empire.

نوری که هرگز خاموش نمی شود
حضرت حسین بن علی سیّد الشّهدا علیه السّلام

FIGURE 5.1

Popular image of Husayn from Iran from a contemporary postcard

The margins of the enormous gateway of the Taj Mahal feature Qur'anic verses describing the garden of paradise at the resurrection; although tourist guidebooks persistently explain this building as the romantic monument to the Mughal emperor's love for his wife, art historians have convincingly argued that it represents the mystical interpretation of the afterlife according to the Sufi metaphysics of Ibn 'Arabi. The spectacular calligraphic decoration of the Alhambra palace in Granada includes not only pious religious formulas but also Arabic court poetry that subtly celebrates the imperial authority of the Moorish ruler. Calligraphy has also conveyed distinctively modern messages, as in a poster from the 1979 Iranian revolution that spells out the Muslim profession of faith ("There is no god but God") with revolutionary raised fists (fig. 5.2).

The immense history of Islamicate art, which can only be hinted at here, includes art produced by and for both Muslims and non-Muslims in ways that complicate and blur the boundaries of religious identity. In fifteenth-century India, a Sanskrit manual for Hindu architects gave instructions on how to build a mosque, described as a temple without images that is dedicated to the formless supreme God; it also appears that Hindu architects who restored the Qutb Minar in Delhi in 1368 had their own theological understanding of the mosque structure.[31] When the Spanish Christian king Pedro the Cruel (also known as Pedro the Just) constructed a new palace in Seville in 1351, he employed workmen from the Moorish kingdom of Granada who filled this monument with Arabic calligraphy and arabesque design. Certainly Pedro was aware of the religious content and implications of these Islamicate design elements. His use of Moorish architectural style seems to have been based on the desire to emulate the most convincing available model of imperial authority rather than on any notion of interreligious

FIGURE 5.2
Muslim profession of faith ("There is no god but God")
spelled out by revolutionary fists on a 1979 poster from Iran

understanding. Despite the centuries-long anti-Muslim Christian militancy of the Spanish Reconquista, Spanish Christians continued to use artistic styles and motifs taken from the Moors, even after their expulsion and forced conversion commencing in 1492. This so-called Mudejar art (the Spanish term is taken from the Arabic word *mudajjan*, meaning a Moorish subject in Christian territory) was a Christian appropriation of Islamicate culture, despite a deep Christian ambivalence about the Islamic faith.[32]

Another form of European appropriation of Islamicate culture came to the fore in the mid-nineteenth century in the school of realistic painting known as Orientalist art. Born at roughly the same time as the new technique of photography, Orientalist painting was the creation of artists (especially but not exclusively in France) who had traveled at least once to North Africa or the Near East. For Europe at that time, Oriental defined the immediate East, which was primarily the Ottoman Empire, viewed as a stand-in for Muslim countries in general. With the growth of printing and the immense popularity of travel literature, pictorial representations of exotic cultures had become a staple of visual illustration. Yet neither the travel books nor the illustrations of faraway countries provided genuine encounters with other cultures. Travelers tended to take with them deeply ingrained prejudices frequently based on the reading of earlier travel books rather than their own observation. Illustrations were often commissioned by publishers, who frequently recycled stock images on the basis of well-established stereotypes. Ironically, works of fantasy were often more eagerly accepted as authentic representations of remote lands. This tendency had been seen in medieval times, when the realistic travel narrative of Marco Polo was generally considered far inferior to the outrageous adventures of Sir John Mandeville, which are filled with tales of encounters with fabulous beasts and monsters. The imagined Orient was a counterimage against which Europe defined itself.

Even before European colonialism established its superiority over the Ottoman Empire and other Muslim regions, European authors took a regal and superior attitude toward the nations of the Orient, as shown by this declaration from an early-eighteenth-century collection of pictures from the Near East: "The reader imagines himself inspecting the other inhabitants of the Earth, and exercising over them a kind of sovereignty, he examines them with attention, approves or condemns their choice of customs, amuses himself and often laughs at the oddness of some, sometimes admires the beauty and majesty of others, always preferring the customs of the country where he was born."[33] The impulse to depict the Orient in visual form received a major boost with Napoleon's expedition to Egypt, which issued ultimately in the publication (1803–28) of the massive *Description de l'Égypte* by a team of French scholars, with numerous maps and illustrations of both ancient and modern Egypt. One of the most striking aspects of the Orientalist imagination was how it collapsed the present into the ancient past, invariably regarding Orientals as trapped in a time warp that prevented them from being part of the present. This powerful metaphor has become an omnipresent cliché in travel writing and journalism; how many times has a writer ponderously observed that visiting the country of X was like traveling back in time 500 years?

Euro-Americans regarded the exotic Muslim Orient from two primary angles. One was the scientific colonial perspective, which forefronted the discoveries of ancient civilizations in Egypt and Mesopotamia. These tableaux of antiquity were seen as canvases of grandeur compared with which the modern residents of those regions were sadly in decline. The scientific impulse of Orientalism expressed itself through a comprehensive identification and classification of the peoples of the East according to their "types," particularly in terms of the racial categories by which Europeans defined the rest of the world. The other point of view was that of Protestant Christian pilgrims, who eagerly sought the places in the Holy Land where the life of Jesus had taken place. In either case, time played strange tricks. Contemporary Arab Bedouin costume was viewed as the equivalent of biblical garb, so that American travelers (who rarely could converse with Arab Christians or Muslims) imagined themselves transported back in time or understood the Near East to exist in a timeless realm unaffected by history. The very real effects of the nineteenth-century version of globalizing trade (of which Euro-American tourism was a manifestation) by then had intimately linked Muslim countries with the economies of Europe and America. Yet these connections were glossed over by powerful images of "East is East, and West is West," as the imperialist poet Kipling put it.

One of the most remarkable aspects of Orientalist art was the erotic fantasy that permeated many paintings. The travelers, usually males, who visited the territories of the Ottoman emperors of course had no access to the women's quarters, which are generally known as the harem or private residence. This was no obstacle to their imagination, however, and there are countless harem scenes filled with dozens of naked women in the bath. Far from being realistic portrayals of Turkish society, these voyeuristic paintings (using nude European models) confused the living quarters with the Turkish bath, and they reduced the Muslim woman to the status of a plaything of unseen Eastern males.[34] Other favorite locations in paintings of Oriental women depicted them for sale in the slave market like so much horseflesh or as dancers performing in front of a male audience; in either case, they were seen as oppressed. The erotic image is the reversal of the stereotype of the veil; the only difference is that the veil has been removed by the imagination. Oriental (i.e., Muslim) men, in the alternate stereotype, were frequently depicted as warriors, whether engaged in fierce battle or in indolent relaxation. These images reinforced the notion of violent Islam while suggesting that these behind-the-times soldiers could be easily conquered.

To be sure, the Orientalist imagination admired the picturesque landscape and the striking individuals whom the painter could observe in the village, the bazaar, or among the ruins of ancient empires. Like romantic paintings of the American West, with their idealized Indians and cowboys, Orientalist paintings of the Islamic East provide a nostalgic access to an imagined past that continues to captivate audiences today. This romantic fascination, aided by Arabian Nights fantasies that still endure in Disney cartoons, soon moved beyond academic art to the realm of popular culture.[35] Novels set in the East (such as Thomas Moore's popular *Lalla Rookh*) were accompanied by Orientalist operas (Mozart's *Abduction from the Seraglio*), comical popular songs ("Ahab the Arab"), and advertisements (Camel cigarettes) with Oriental settings. Dressing up in Oriental costume ("harem pants") was highly fashionable with the upper classes and became the uniform for Masonic societies like the Shriners. Fairs such as the Columbian Exposition of 1898 introduced American audiences to mockups of Egyptian villages and to belly-dancing. Films like *The Sheik*, with Rudolf Valentino, and *The Thief of Baghdad*, with Douglas Fairbanks, further entrenched the fantastic images of the Muslim East. The main images in Hollywood films revolved around the eroticism of the imagined Near Eastern female form and the dangerous violence of the Arab.[36] In an eerie parallel with the film depiction of American Indians, Hollywood Arabs became increasingly identified with violence standing in the way of civilization. The apogee of this sensational depiction of fanatic Muslims is seen in fantasies such as *True Lies*, with Arnold Schwarzenegger, where mindless violence is shown as synonymous with Islam. All these are examples of Euro-American artistic representations of Islam and Islamicate culture through the imagination. The distinguishing feature of the Orientalist impulse, whether in fine art or popular culture, is the use of the foreignness of the Oriental as a contrast to define the civilization of the so-called West as the opposite of barbarism.

Another question regarding Islamicate art arises when we turn to the realm of modern art as an international phenomenon.[37] The lines between traditional art forms can become blurred simply by the introduction of new physical media, as when oil paints were adopted in Iran in the nineteenth century; suddenly, murals and new kinds of portraiture replaced the Persian miniature styles of the past.[38] Yet even in modern media such as film, there can also be distinctive artistic approaches reflecting local sensibilities. Recent Iranian films such as *Gabbeh*, depicting love and beauty among the nomadic tribes of southern Persia with lyrical intensity, or *The Color of Paradise*, with its rich evocation of the spirituality of children, radically depart from Hollywood styles of filmmaking. On the other hand, there are modern Bangladeshi artists whose abstract compositions would be hard to distinguish from the production of contemporary artists from Japan or the Netherlands. A recent publication of works by contemporary women artists from Iran refuses to fit into any neat categories (especially since many of the artists leave their works untitled).[39] An example is a watercolor titled *Ascension*, by Feeroozeh Golmohammadi (fig. 5.3). Her painting contains "details reminiscent of Persian themes—the costumes, headgear, prayer beads, and the phoenix-like bird at the bottom. Her imagery and mystical theme is similar in style and content to the work of the twentieth-century German artist Sulamith Wülfing as well as the contemporary popular New Age artist Susan Seddon Boulet. This is not to suggest that Golmo-hammadi's painting is derivative. Instead, this similarity of styles exemplifies how images, as well as ideas, are now globally available and an increasingly shared medium."[40] The extent to which these artistic productions can be called Islamicate is hard to determine, particularly since many of them partake of global trends in artistic media and conception.

These different aspects of what may loosely be called Islamic art testify to centuries of development of the sense of beauty within Muslim cultures. Even the European appropriation and objectification of Islamic art and the participation of Muslims in international modern art still engage the aesthetic dimension of artistic creativity. But a powerful counterimpulse has arisen in certain extreme manifestations of Islamist ideology in recent years that would abolish the sense of beauty altogether from Muslim societies. The most prominent intellectual exponents of this extreme iconoclastic trend are undoubtedly the proponents of the Wahhabi ideology that emerged from Arabia in the nineteenth century and which has gained a certain amount of acceptance among other highly conservative groups that do not consider themselves Wahhabis. Current authorities of this school, such as Shaykh al-Baz in Saudi Arabia, have called for a total ban on images of any kind, extending even to the prohibition of photographs in family albums. In part, this rejection of images should be seen in the context of the deep ambivalence generated by global advertising, with its heavy reliance on sex to sell everything one can imagine. To protect their control over the social order, the constituents of the Wahhabi movement and allied groups define sexuality through rigid delimitations of separate spaces for males and females. Somehow the alienation of the feminine from public spaces appears to be linked with the extreme rejection of visual images.

Most dramatically, the Taliban of Afghanistan demonstrated

FIGURE 5.3
Ascension, *by Feeroozeh Golmohammadi*
(*from* Manifestation of Feeling: A Selection of Painting
by Iranian Female Artists *[Tehran: Center for Visual Arts,
Ministry of Culture and Islamic Guidance, 1995], 89)*

their extreme abhorrence of images when they destroyed the colossal Buddhas of Bamiyan that had stood in Afghanistan since the time of Alexander. The demolition of these statues was only the most spectacular event in a campaign of destruction that reduced the irreplaceable contents of the Kabul Museum to rubble. In a stroke the Taliban annihilated (or sold on the black market) more than 2,000 years of treasures from the many cultures that traversed the Silk Road. They also proclaimed their unprecedented austerity by outlawing all photographs (except identity cards) and all forms of music except recitation of the Qur'an. Meanwhile, organs of the Saudi government have echoed the iconoclastic policy of tomb destruction by demolishing, under the euphemistic formula of renovation, Ottoman-era buildings in Arabia that do not fit their austere definition of art. They have also succeeded, using the same logic, in destroying Ottoman mosques in Bosnia that had survived Serbian attack during the Yugoslavian civil war.[41] Astonishingly, this new breed of Islamists declares that all forms of beauty—even geometric ornament, vegetal arabesque, and calligraphy—must be banished from the earth. Doubtless the Taliban feel a great attraction in resisting the powerful and enticing advertising images with which globalizing business floods the world. But the abolition of images by Wahhabis and their allies comes at the cost of renouncing both beauty and spirituality.

CHAPTER 6
POSTSCRIPT
REIMAGINING ISLAM
IN THE
TWENTY-FIRST CENTURY

Beyond East and West

The most common contemporary concept of Islam is based on the dynamics and inner drives of recent history, particularly the colonial period. Far from representing an eternal and unchanging essence, Islam is a symbol that has shifted in meaning as different actors have appropriated it. In Europe and America, Islam is still understood through relentlessly colonial attitudes that are often combined with a near-total amnesia about the history of colonialism. This climate of opinion provides the unsuspecting with a persuasive portrait of the West as the apex of civilization. Those who fall outside the West are viewed either as opponents of progress or as part of an undeveloped culture whose ultimate destiny is to become like the West. Although one hopes that the age of outright colonial domination has passed, colonial attitudes persist in the economic globalization that markets the products of Europe and the United States to the rest of the world. Colonial attitudes continue to underlie even the well-meaning theories of development and modernization that are institutionalized in foreign aid policies and nongovernmental organizations. In these circumstances, significant cultural differences are seen as potential impediments to the rational spread of a homogeneous civilization.

The identification of "the West" with advanced science and technology confers an intoxicating sense of superiority on its beneficiaries, so that even those of us who find it difficult to program a VCR still consider ourselves the proprietary owners of modern science. The doctrine of progress places less technological societies further back on the timeline of advancement, so that tourists and armchair travelers can marvel at the prospect of countries that are stuck in a time several centuries ago. The power of this metaphor of technological progress on a timeline can blind us to the fact that people in countries with less technology are still our contemporaries. Even people who plow by water buffalo or drive horse carts today are part of the contemporary world—and in their village there may be a television on which they watch MTV. Forcing ourselves to acknowledge this apparently simple fact may also help us become aware of the many relationships—economic, political, and cultural—that have joined Euro-America with the so-called East for many years.

In the nineteenth century, colonial thinking opposed the scientific West to the superstitious East, which was thought to be still mired in medieval times. Some Asian thinkers sought to turn this stereotype on its head by proclaiming the East the home of spirituality and the West the abode of soulless materialism. As an anticolonial rallying cry, this position has had considerable appeal until the present day, and leaders and ideologues from Gandhi to Khomeini have invoked it with great success. But there are serious conceptual problems in the opposition of East and West, Asia and Europe, Orient and Occident. One of the supporters of the idea of the spiritual East was Indian poet Rabindranath Tagore, who won the Nobel Prize for literature in 1912. Tagore attempted to take his message of Asian spirituality to China and Japan to seek solidarity for his India-based critique of the West. To his surprise, he found that the Chinese and Japanese had no patience for his notion of spirituality, which they found obscure and impractical. Instead, they were seeking to bootstrap their industrial and military establishments to withstand the economic and political aggression of Europe and the United States.[1]

Where, indeed, is the East? Asia, originally a Greek term for the lands to the east (Asia Minor was the coast of modern Turkey), has become a very elastic and relative concept. Most Americans think of Asia and the Orient as China, Japan, and neighboring countries, despite the fact that they lie to the west of America. Is Japan now part of the West because of its advanced economy? If so, South Korea, China, and Malaysia may not be far behind, but East and West will have lost any geographic significance by then. The cultural definition of Western civilization as the heritage of Hebrew prophecy and Greek philosophy has already been shown to be problematic, since these are the sources of Islamic civilization as well. Yet in numerical terms, Islam is the largest Asian religion, with more followers than either Hinduism or Buddhism. Unless we wish to retain the colonial attitude, it seems absurd to retain the opposition of East and West, since the reality is that people of all nations today are intertwined in the same processes and experiences. If we simply want to describe major economic divisions, there are alternative terms. The use of North and South to indicate the industrialized economies and the poor countries of the world is an attempt to point out this dichotomy, but without the ideological and colonial implications of East and West. Since East and West carry so much historical baggage, those who have second thoughts about colonial attitudes may wish to dispense with them once and for all.

Similarly, it should be acknowledged that an extreme form of Islamic ideology underlies the recent emergence of terrorist networks that have organized attacks on centers of American political, military, and economic power. While it is technically correct to say that this Islamic extremism occurs in the context of colonialism and globalization, that historical explanation should not be construed as an excuse for criminal acts of violence.[2] The encouragement of fanatical hatred of a monolithic and satanic West is a distorted view of history that serves a savage will to power. For the minority of Muslim ideologues who wage an apocalyptic struggle against godless Europe and America, the lives of innocent civilians and of willing foot soldiers are equally expendable. The rhetoric of Islam against the West, from this perspective, too, can only lead to confrontation and violence. The perpetuation of an extremist anticolonial mentality in Muslim societies will continue to jeopardize the ethical values that underlie Islamic tradition.

New Images of Islam

The effect of colonialism on the concept of Islam has been to re-arrange priorities and religious identities worldwide, because of the us-versus-them character of colonial ideologies. Through the new communications technologies unleashed by globalization, Islam became a badge of transnational solidarity against European invaders. In the nineteenth century, nationalism spread as a concept of "imagined community" by which people identified themselves as part of a theoretical society that joined them to multitudes of strangers. In an analogous way, advocates of the transnational concept of Islam gave that notion priority over concrete local communities, despite the ethnic, cultural, and linguistic diversity of those communities. As the chief contender with Christianity for religious domination of the globe, the reformist concept of Islam was also taking on the character of a religion in the European sense, partly in response to the attacks of Christian missionaries. Colonial authorities interpreted Islamic personal law in ways that were much narrower and more restrictive than premodern Muslim judicial systems. Post-colonial advocates of Islamic government used the mechanisms of the modern nation-state to implement inflexible new codes of unprecedented harshness in the guise of restoring the pristine Islamic law of an idealized Medina at the time of the Prophet.

The process of redefining Islam as ideology has proceeded unabated, with sometimes surprising results. This ideological concept of Islam requires activism to overturn undesirable situations, particularly the imposition of colonial foreign rule and its successor, the secular state. This ideological activism requires the transformation of Islam into a very political tool, objectifying it into a thing that is instrumental to the attainment of other ends. The radical innovation of this ideological notion of Islam was brought home to me forcefully in a conversation with an Iranian American student in California some years ago. We were discussing the prominent Shi'i theologian Ayatollah Khu'i, who resided in Iraq. "He is only a religious mullah," observed the student, "because he does not really talk about Islam." What was astonishing about this remark was the way it dismissed a major religious scholar on the grounds that he was not an ideological activist; the fact that his work concentrated on traditional ethics, ritual, and interpretation of authoritative texts made him irrelevant to the transnational political concerns of the student. Most remarkably, the term "Islam" had shifted into an almost entirely political register.

Another surprising definition of Islam comes from Pakistan, which since its founding in 1947 has struggled to define itself as an Islamic state. One of the most contentious issues among the many sectarian disputes that have troubled the state has been the status of the Ahmadi sect. This group has tested the boundaries of orthodoxy because of claims that the nineteenth-century founder, Mirza Ghulam Ahmad, could have been a prophet after Muhammad (many Muslims regard the prophethood of Muhammad as the final revelation, so that any claimant to prophecy is typically looked upon with great suspicion). In 1974 the government of President Z. A. Bhutto passed a law that declared Ahmadis (also called Qadianis) to be non-Muslims. Subsequent challenges to this law, on the basis of fundamental rights guaranteed by Pakistan's constitution, succeeded in calling this law into question.

A major reversal took place, however, in a 1993 judicial decision that perhaps for the first time in history actually spelled out a detailed governmental definition of Islam. The presiding judge declared that the symbols and rites of Islam (such as the profession of faith, and buildings called mosques) were the equivalent of intellectual property that could be copyrighted by the rightful owners, although he never spelled out just how such claims of ownership could be established. Therefore anyone who improperly recited the profession of faith or called their place of worship a mosque was in effect using a copyrighted logo without permission and was liable to legal penalties.[3] The implications of this decision are breathtaking. Not only is a religion being defined as a commodity or piece of property, which the judge actually compared to Coca-Cola, but also the courts—not religious communities—are entitled to decide what is essential to any religion.[4] Moreover, in this decision the limits of Islam are being defined in relation to a modern sectarian group. Current Pakistani passports now require professed Muslim citizens to sign a declaration that they adhere to the finality of the prophethood of Muhammad—that is, that they are not Ahmadis. Such an outcome (reminiscent of oaths of orthodox interpretation of Holy Communion during the Protestant Reformation) can only be imagined as a result of very recent local history.

We are left with a confusing situation, particularly in terms of the many concepts of religion described earlier in this book. By "Islam" do we mean the scriptural definition of performing the basic ritual actions that denote submission to God (profession of faith, ritual prayer, fasting in Ramadan, giving alms, and pilgrimage)? If so, should we restrict the term "Islam" to the level of minimum conformity with the expectations of a particular Muslim community? That would follow classical theologians such as Ghazali, who considered that membership in the Muslim community applies to anyone who prays toward Mecca (although in practice he took serious issue with philosophers and Shi'is over their theologies). But the problem with any authoritative definition of religion remains the same: Who is entitled to define Islam? In any society in the world today, religious pluralism is a sociological fact. If one group claims authority over all the rest, demanding their allegiance and submission, this will be experienced as the imposition of power through religious rhetoric.

There will always be a gap between the prescriptive, normative, ideal concept of religion and the descriptive, historical, and sociological accounts of religion. In contrast to the authoritative declarations of theologians and the apparatus of the nation-state, scholars and other outsiders have to be content with a much broader notion of what can be considered Islamic. In this sense, we could describe as Islamic a number of competing theologies that are based on the Qur'an. We could include various ethical systems (including basic rituals) that appeal to Muhammad as a model of behavior. Among other Islamic institutions would be the many important lineages of charismatic spiritual transmission, whether Sufi or Shi'i, and a variety of local practices such as pilgrimage to shrines. Rituals of the life cycle, such as birth, marriage, and death, would also fall into the category of Islamic. The extended range of culture associated with Islamic religion, covering such aspects of life as music, poetry, art, architecture, and government, can be regarded in a related sense as Islamicate.

But neither practice nor belief as the definition of religion has much to do with the modern objectification of religion, the tendency to view religion as a thing with fixed essential characteristics. One of the great innovations of Islamist reform has been to introduce the notion of Islam as a totalizing system that controls all aspects of public and private life. Expressed by oft-repeated slogans ("There is no separation of politics from religion in Islam" or "Islam is not just a religion, but a way of life"), this new concept of Islam was argued with the techniques of Protestant Christianity, appealed to scriptural authority, and rejected centuries of historical tradition. Muslim fundamentalists made the tactical decision to deploy all the resources of modern globalizing media technology to communicate their antimodernist message, in this way leveraging a platform they could never command on their own. What is most remarkable about the spread of this new image of Islam is not the successful inroads of this ideology among traditional Muslim populations, where it remains a minority view. The real surprise is, instead, the successful and overwhelming triumph of this view of Islam among non-Muslims. Through the uncritical broadcast of fundamentalist screeds by well-meaning but uninformed media outlets, Islamist ideology has managed to be the only form of Islam that most non-Muslims have ever encountered. In a huge irony, the gift of the Protestant principle of scriptural authority has been returned with interest, as Islamists convert most of their opponents to a fundamentalist interpretation of Islam.

One unsuspected corollary of this ideological approach to Islam has been the identification of the Islamic religion with particular political regimes or empires. While this identification has doubtless been encouraged by rulers who claim religious legitimacy, there are serious problems in merging religion with particular governments. For one thing, when Saddam Hussein or Yasser Arafat calls upon the authority of Islam to buttress his political positions, it should be recalled that he has fewer religious credentials than American politicians such as Richard Nixon. On a more profound level, if history has taught us anything, it is that the rise and fall of empires has no moral meaning in itself, nor does superior military technology confer civilizational advancement. Although there is an understandable human desire for winners to interpret victory as divine favor, there are few who would candidly agree that military conquest is equivalent to moral supremacy.

Beyond this moral issue, there are further conceptual problems with politicizing religion. If Islam is incarnated in governments rather than in people, does "Islam" mean only countries with Muslim majorities or Muslim-majority-countries-plus-countries-with-significant-Muslim-minorities? If one considers only Muslim majority countries that call Islam the state religion, one excludes countries with explicitly secular constitutions, such as Indonesia (the largest Muslim country), Turkey, and the former Soviet republics. On closer examination, even countries that call themselves Islamic republics have composite structures. Their hybrid legal systems replace theoretical Islamic law with appeals to Islamic authority, recast in the legal codes of nation-states that also draw on colonial law, local custom, and administrative decree.

The images of Islam that have dominated the past two centuries were generated in a context of conflict, either/or, and East against West. These were images without dialogue, which like Orientalist painting, defined Euro-American culture in contrast to the exotic other. Yet Muslims around the world, like it or not, have been engaged with the main issues of modernity throughout this same period when they have been defined as nonmodern, non-Western, and noncivilized. Muslims have been debating the same questions that have agitated Europeans and Americans: women's rights, human rights, Marxism, nationalism, revolution, democracy, and now globalization. Remarkably, the terms most often used to demonize Muslims have arisen within the heart of Euro-American modernity. It was the French Revolution that gave birth to the words "terrorism" and "fanaticism," and American Protestantism brought forth "fundamentalism." The momentum and the aftershocks of colonialism will probably continue on the international stage for some time.

What will the new images of Islam look like? The growing presence of educated Muslim minorities in America and Europe will be the decisive ingredient that will finally make possible a true dialogue that can create new images for a single world in which both Muslims and non-Muslims exist. Some of this dialogue will doubtless take place through debates that attempt to locate the sources of Islamic tradition in relation to contemporary issues. Yet the effort to create new images for a single world has been under way for many years. Perhaps the chief resource, still largely unrecognized, is the creative activity of Muslims, particularly in the form of the novel, a distinctively European literary form that has been widely practiced in Muslim majority countries for more than a century. Muslims have certainly been using other artistic media such as music (hip-hop, rai, beur, and other genres) to reflect on contemporary issues. But the novel, with its psychological reflection and sociological commentary, is perhaps the best source for realistic depiction of the lives of Muslims.[5] In these writings, in contrast with ideological presentations, Islam turns out to be one thread interwoven with the rest of life, as in a tapestry, but there are many other issues that undergo examination; secular issues, politics, class, gender relations, colonialism, and local history make up the substance of most of these narratives. It is to these creative forms that we should look for the elaboration of the new images of Islam that will frame our future.

One more aspect of modernity that needs to be considered as a source of new images of Islam is technology, particularly in the field of communications. This process began initially with the shift from hand production of manuscripts to the printed book, and it soon proceeded to other forms of communication, including radio and television, cassette tapes, and the Internet. In European history it is commonly observed that the Protestant Reformation was to a certain extent the child of print; Gutenberg's invention of movable type made possible the first modern best-seller, Martin Luther's German translation of the Bible. Print put the sacred text into the hands of the ordinary believer, thus empowering the individual to interpret scripture without license from the church. For a variety of reasons that are still disputed, it was not until the nineteenth century that printing became a major factor in the dissemination of Islamic sacred texts. Here, too, the new media of print made it possible to deliver copies of scripture and other religious writings to unprecedented numbers of literate believers, and groups ranging from Islamists to Sufis have made full use of this medium to spread their messages.

The most recent forms of communications technology, particularly the Internet, have introduced new dynamics into the notion of religious community associated with Islam.[6] Texts are being published on the Internet as authoritative sources for guidance on all aspects of behavior. Some Islamic websites, loaded with extensive texts, graphics, and links, are comprehensive vehicles for virtual communities where new forms of personal interaction are carried out and mediated by the technology itself. One of the most remarkable aspects of the new technology is the use of email for religious questions that can be answered by teams of experts, in an "Ask the Imam" format. With complete anonymity, Muslims are able to ask questions about the most intimate matters of personal behavior, and they receive rulings from a wide range of authoritative positions. In addition, sectarian minority groups are able to publish their positions with considerable freedom. Although it is too soon to say what the effects of these technologies will be, it appears likely that multiple voices will be able to contribute their own distinctive accounts of Islam to global audiences.

Islam and Pluralism

The historical argument set forth in this book suggests that Islam has never meant one thing, nor will it in the future. History reveals multiple interpretive authorities clustered around core texts and practices, with variations manifest in local traditions. Modern communications and the new concept of Islam as an anticolonial ideology have made it appealing to invoke the idea of Muslim unity. Dissident views are discouraged as fractures in the universal community of Muslims. Distinctive local practices are frowned upon as deviations from a homogeneous norm. Yet who is entitled to decide what Islam is, once and for all?

At the same time that globalizing communications have opened up the possibility of a monolithic Islamist discourse, previously unheard voices are now being heard. Among the new developments is a reevaluation of tradition by feminists, including Islamist women. While it will be tempting for development-minded Euro-American feminists to view their own trajectory as the only possible model for Muslim women, they will need to resist that assumption if they wish to hear the voices of their Muslim sisters. We are likewise now able to hear the voices of Muslim minority groups, including those who have been dismissed as sectarian heretics. Countries that define themselves as Islamic states are wrestling with the questions of the rights of women and the rights of religious minorities as human rights issues. These debates about pluralism will answer not only to local constituencies but also to international scrutiny through the media.

For non-Muslims, the larger question remains whether there can be a tolerance of pluralistic ethics. All ethical systems contain elements of both reason and authority, but it is tempting particularly for modern Europeans and Americans to regard their own ethical ideals (or the idealized versions of their societies) as both rational and universal. The possibility that there might be elements of irrationality, injustice, or the force of custom in our society is not often entertained directly. Democracy, for instance, is generally regarded as the highest form of government, containing in itself the elements of virtue. We tend to forget that democracy in the United States has evolved over time; that it originally excluded women, slaves, and the poor; and that its application even today is not without problems. As shown earlier, the resources of Islamic ethics (whether scriptural, philosophical, or local) cover a broad range of activities from ritual purity to diet, family relations, and government. As Augustine pointed out in his analysis of religion, it is the historical dimension of revelation that allows a distinctive dispensation for particular times and places. Muslims will continue to make their ethical decisions in a context of both Islamic scriptural resources (Qur'an and hadith) and external traditions (Greek philosophy and modern European thought). Will Euro-Americans be able to tolerate the existence of a distinctively Islamic dispensation within their midst? Whatever their differences, will Muslims be permitted, like Jews and Christians, to raise questions of ethics and social justice based on their own traditions? That will be another test of pluralism in the future.

If the distinctiveness of the Islamic tradition, like any other religious tradition, derives from the historical dimension of revelation, then we are more than ever confronted with the centrality of Muhammad. Yet the unity of Islamic revelation, manifest in the Qur'an, the Prophet, and the central ritual of Meccan pilgrimage, is also refracted by history and locality. Muslims will undoubtedly continue to debate whether this prophetic heritage is a system that can be seized and implemented by authoritative decree or whether it is to be continually renegotiated on the basis of individual responsibility. Muslim thinkers have speculated about the question of Muhammad's authority for many years. On one hand, he said, "Difference of opinion is a mercy for my community." Yet on the other hand, he stated, "My community will never agree upon error." In the effort to work out inconsistencies, some resort to the technical expedient of rejecting these hadith on the basis of traditional criticism of the transmitters. Among the casualties of this process are the writings of major figures such as al-Ghazali; notorious for employing "weak" hadith, his writings have been recently republished in expurgated form, with all questionable quotations from the Prophet removed or marked as suspicious. Yet for al-Ghazali and generations of his successors, the wisdom of the Prophet was clearly greater than the narrowest scholarly canon.

Who has the authority to define Islam? The pragmatic pluralism of historical times and places works against the will to power that would reduce Islam to a single voice. An analogy would be the ritual process of determining the beginning of the sacred month of Ramadan, which is done by the physical sighting of the moon. In practice, because of differing weather conditions, this means that even in fairly close localities, people might differ about exactly when Ramadan begins. Following Muhammad, like the sighting of that moon, is the responsibility of those who consider themselves Muslims. It is the responsibility of non-Muslims to acknowledge the legitimacy of that enterprise.

NOTES

Chapter One

Arabic epigraph: From the "Light Verse" of the Qur'an (24:35) (epigraph portion marked in italics): "God is the light of the heavens and earth. The likeness of his light is as a niche, in which there is a lamp. The lamp in a glass—the glass as though it were a shining star—is *kindled from a blessed tree, an olive that is neither of the east nor west,* the oil of which nearly lights up without fire touching it. It is light upon light. God guides by his light those whom he wishes. God speaks to humanity in similitudes; God is knowing with all things."

1. In 1999 the languages with the largest total number of speakers were the following (in millions): Mandarin Chinese, 1,075; English, 514; Hindi-Urdu, 496; Spanish, 425; Arabic, 256; Bengali, 215; Portuguese, 194; Malay-Indonesian, 179; French, 129; German, 128; Japanese, 126 (*The World Almanac and Book of Facts, 1999*).

2. Samuel P. Huntington, "The Clash of Civilizations," *Foreign Affairs* 72, no. 3 (Summer 1993): 22–28; Samuel P. Huntington, *The Clash of Civilizations and the Remaking of World Order* (New York: Simon and Schuster, 1996). As of November 2001, Huntington's book was the number 18 best-seller on Amazon.com.

3. For an insightful analysis of the destructive consequences of assuming that there are multiple worlds in conflict, see Eric Voegelin, "World-Empire and the Unity of Mankind," in *Published Essays, 1953–1965,* ed. Ellis Sandoz (Columbia: University of Missouri Press, 2000), 134–55. For a cogent argument against the "clash of civilizations" theory, see Fred Halliday, *Islam and the Myth of Confrontation: Religion and Politics in the Middle East,* rev. ed. (London: I. B. Tauris, 2002).

4. For a comprehensive documentation of the broader relations of Europe with Asia, see Donald F. Lach and Edwin J. Van Kley, *Asia in the Making of Europe,* 3 vols. (Chicago: University of Chicago Press, 1965–93).

5. Sir Charles N. E. Eliot (former diplomat in Russia and Constantinople and colonial official in East Africa, 1888–1904), "Asia: History," in *Encyclopaedia Britannica*, 11th ed. (1910), 2:749–55 (excerpts).

6. Older spellings of the name of the Prophet (Mohammed, Mahomet) should be rejected in favor of the more correct spelling, Muhammad.

7. Writing in 1836, Edward Lane appears to have been the first European author to introduce the word "Islam" as the name of a religion: "The Mohammadan religion is generally called by the Arabs, el-Islám" (*Manners and Customs of the Modern Egyptians* [London, 1836], 1:71). This is clearly a tentative move, because Lane still retains the definite article "el-" (equivalent to the English word "the") in front of the word "Islam," preserving its foreign flavor. Lane seems to have become more sensitive about avoiding the word "Mohammadan," because in the fifth edition of this work, published in 1860, the same sentence reads as follows: "The religion which Mohammad taught is generally called by the Arabs 'El-Islam'" (p. 65). I am grateful to Jason Thompson of the American University in Cairo for providing these citations.

8. For a comprehensive survey of European images of Islam, see the works of Norman Daniel, particularly *Islam and the West: The Making of an Image* (Oxford: Oneworld, 1993), and *Islam, Europe, and Empire* (Edinburgh: Edinburgh University Press, 1966).

9. The "Declaration on the Relation of the Church to Non-Christian Religions" is available online at
⟨http://www.vatican.va/archive/hist_councils/ii_vatican_council/
documents/vat-ii_decl_19651028_nostra-aetate_en.html⟩.

10. Hans Küng, Josef Van Ess, Heinrich von Stietencron, and Heinz Bechert, *Christianity and World Religions: Paths of Dialogue with Islam, Hinduism, and Buddhism* (Garden City, N.Y.: Doubleday, 1986).

11. For many years the most influential work on Muhammad in English was Humphrey Prideaux's *The True Nature of Imposture Fully Display'd in the Life of Mahomet* (London, 1697).

12. An instructive example is the massive book of Richard Knolles, *The generall historie of the Turkes, from the first beginning of that nation to the rising of the Othoman familie; with all the notable expeditions of the Christian princes against them* (London: A. Islip, 1603). This went through numerous editions and was very popular in the next two centuries.

13. See the extensive resources on Kipling's poem and "Anti-Imperial-

ism in America, 1898–1935," collected by Jim Zwick, available online at ⟨http://www.boondocksnet.com/ai/kipling/⟩.

14. Nikki R. Keddie, *An Islamic Response to Imperialism: Political and Religious Writings of Sayyid Jamal ad-Din "al-Afghani"* (Berkeley: University of California Press, 1968). The name al-Afghani was a pseudonym that permitted Jamal al-Din to pass as a Sunni Muslim, although he was originally born a Shi'i in Iran.

15. The full text of Macaulay's Minute is available at ⟨http://www.tc.umn.edu/~raley/research/english/macaulay.html⟩.

16. William Muir, *The life of Mahomet and history of Islam to the era of the Hegira*, 4 vols. (London: Smith, Elder & Co., 1858), 2:xxi–xxii (epilepsy), 91–96 (satanic influence). This text has been made available on a Christian anti-Muslim website (answering-islam.org) and has also been recently reprinted by Voice of India, an anti-Muslim fundamentalist Hindu press in India.

17. See, as an example, W. W. Hunter, *The Indian Musalmans: Are they bound in conscience to rebel against the Queen?* (London, 1871; reprint, Lahore: Premier Book House, 1974). In this case Hunter concluded that Indian Muslims could still be good British subjects.

18. Edward Said, *Orientalism* (New York: Pantheon, 1978).

19. See the perceptive and judicious comments of Jacques Waardenburg in his article on the Orientalists in *Encyclopaedia of Islam* (Leiden: E. J. Brill, 1960–), 7:735–53, under the title "Mustashrikun."

20. On apocalyptic beliefs regarding Jerusalem, see Gershom Gorenberg, *The End of Days: Fundamentalism and the Struggle for the Temple Mount* (New York: Oxford University Press, 2002).

21. See the reports of the Runnymede Trust Commission, "The Future of Multi-Ethnic Britain" and "Islamophobia," available online at ⟨http://www.runnymedetrust.org/meb/index.html⟩.

22. Chibli Mallat, "The Middle East in the Twenty-first Century: An Agenda for Reform," lecture delivered at the School of Oriental and African Studies, October 22, 1996 (available online at ⟨http://www.soas.ac.uk/Centres/IslamicLaw/21st.html⟩).

23. See the useful remarks by Robert Harris, "Evaluating Internet Research Sources" (⟨http://www.virtualsalt.com/evalu8it.htm⟩).

Chapter Two

Arabic epigraph: From the Andalusian Sufi master Ibn 'Arabi: "I follow the religion of love; wherever its camels turn, love is my religion and my faith." As Ibn 'Arabi notes in his own commentary on this verse, "This applies especially to the followers of Muhammad, since Muhammad (God bless him and give him peace), out of all the rest of the prophets, possessed the station of love in its perfection" (*Tarjuman al-ashwaq* [Beirut: Dar Sadir, 1966], 44). By "followers of Muhammad" Ibn 'Arabi does not mean the average believer, however; this verse addresses the advanced soul whose heart is "receptive of every form," who has attained "the station of no station" (William Chittick, *The Sufi Path of Knowledge* [Albany: State University of New York Press, 1989], 376–77).

1. The abbreviation B.C.E., standing for "before the common era," has been adopted by scholars of religious studies to describe a universal chronology that is not exclusively based on a Christian perspective. In this sense, the "common era" (C.E.) coincides with the Gregorian calendar, but it avoids the theological expressions B.C. ("before Christ") and A.D. ("in the year of our Lord"), since it is used by non-Christians as well as Christians.

2. There is another Latin derivation proposed by the early Christian writer Lactantius that relates *religio* to the Latin verb *religare*, "to bind together," suggesting a theological concept of binding together God with humanity. This theological concept was missing, however, in the pre-Christian use of the word. For a detailed study, see Wilfred Cantwell Smith, *The Meaning and End of Religion: A New Approach to the Religious Traditions of Mankind* (New York: Macmillan, 1963; reprint, Minneapolis: Fortress Press, 1991), which forms the basis for a number of comments here.

3. Hugo Grotius, *True Religion Explained and Defended against ye Archenemies Thereof in These Times* (London, 1632), 99.

4. Justice Arthur Goldberg in Schempp (1963), in Charles C. Haynes and Oliver Thomas, *Finding Common Ground: A First Amendment Guide to Religion and Public Education,* 3rd ed. (Nashville, Tenn.: First Amendment Center, 1998), 4.8 (available online at
‹http://www.freedomforum.org/templates/
document.asp?documentID=3979›).

5. On the objectification of Islam in recent times, see Dale F. Eickelman

and James Piscatori, *Muslim Politics* (Princeton: Princeton University Press, 1996), esp. chap. 2.

6. Russell McCutcheon, "The Category 'Religion' in Recent Publications: A Critical Survey," *Numen* 42 (1995): 284–309.

7. Thomas A. Tweed, "Night-Stand Buddhists and Other Creatures: Sympathizers, Adherents, and the Study of Religion," in *American Buddhism: Methods and Findings in Recent Scholarship*, ed. Duncan Ryuken Williams and Christopher S. Queen (Surrey, U.K.: Curzon Press, 1999), 71–90.

8. For a perceptive and thoughtful discussion of problems of defining religious membership and categories of religion, see the "Frequently Asked Questions" section of the website ‹http://www.adherents.com/›.

9. The comprehensive modern Persian encyclopedia of 'Ali Akbar Dihkhuda, *Lughat nama*, gives four possible derivations for the word *musalman*: (1) a term of humility meaning "resembling a Muslim" (*muslim-man*; while found in several medieval dictionaries, this derivation is rejected by Dihkhuda on linguistic grounds); (2) a plural of the Arabic *muslim*, mistakenly turned into a singular by Persians; (3) a term taken from the name of the Prophet's disciple Salman the Persian, which the Persians adopted as a badge of pride in the face of Arab ethnocentrism; and (4) a derogatory form of *muslim* applied by Arabs to Persians, who unwittingly accepted the term. It is remarkable that only the first derivation, rejected by the modern editor, has a mainly religious significance; the rest are all colored by ethnic and historical considerations. *Musalman* is still in use in Turkish, Persian, Urdu, and even European languages such as Spanish and French.

10. For an instructive interpretation of Islam based around this "*hadith* of Gabriel," see Sachiko Murata and William C. Chittick, *The Vision of Islam* (St. Paul, Minn.: Paragon House, 1995).

11. Marshall G. S. Hodgson, *The Venture of Islam: Conscience and History in a World Civilization*, 3 vols. (Chicago: University of Chicago Press, 1974).

12. For an important critical analysis of Salafi and Wahhabi thought, see Khaled Abou El Fadl, "The Ugly Modern and the Modern Ugly: Reclaiming the Beautiful in Islam," in *Progressive Muslims on Gender, Justice, and Pluralism*, ed. Omid Safi (Oxford: Oneworld, 2003), 33–78.

13. Bruce B. Lawrence, *Defenders of God: The Fundamentalist Revolt against the Modern Age* (Charleston: University of South Carolina Press, 1995).

14. Martin E. Marty and R. Scott Appleby, eds., *The Fundamentalism Project*, 5 vols. (Chicago: University of Chicago Press, 1994–95).

Chapter Three

Arabic epigraph: "We only sent you as *a mercy for creation*" (Qur'an 21:107). This verse, in which God addresses the Prophet Muhammad, is a fundamental Qur'anic statement about the universal role of the Prophet.

1. Jalal al-Din Muhammad Balkhi, *Mathnawi*, 6 vols., ed. with commentary by Muhammad Isti'lami (Tehran: Zavvar, 1991), 1:9 (bk. 1, verse 6).

2. For standard biographies, see Maxime Rodinson, *Muhammad*, trans. Anne Carter (New York: New Press, 2002); Michael Cook, *Muhammad* (Oxford: Oxford University Press, 1993).

3. Annemarie Schimmel, *And Muhammad Is His Messenger: The Veneration of the Prophet in Islamic Piety* (Chapel Hill: University of North Carolina Press, 1985), 34, citing Tirmidhi, *Kitab shama'il al-Mustafa.*

4. Text from double *hilya* composition by Rasheed Butt, permanent collection of Ackland Art Museum, University of North Carolina at Chapel Hill, my translation. For a fuller description of this double composition, and examples in color, see

⟨http://www.rasheedbutt.com/igallery.cfm?start=2⟩.

5. Schimmel, *And Muhammad Is His Messenger*, 36, citing Tirmidhi. For additional *hilya* images (*hilye* in Turkish), see Huseyin Gunduz and Faruk Taskale, *Dancing Letters: A Selection of Turkish Calligraphic Art*, trans. Mujde Odabasıoglu (Istanbul: Antik Inc. Co. Publications, 2000), ⟨http://www.antikpalace.com.tr/antikas/dancingletters.html⟩. The Turkish Ministry of Foreign Affairs, interestingly, has a website with more *hilya* examples and information at

⟨http://www.mfa.gov.tr/grupc/cj/cja/holydesc.htm⟩.

6. For examples of contemporary Shi'i biographies of Muhammad, see Mohammad Baqir as-Sadr, *The Revealer, the Messenger, the Message*, trans. Mahmoud M. Ayoub (Tehran: World Organization for Islamic Services, 1980), ⟨http://al-islam.org/revealer/⟩; Sayyid Mujtaba Musavi Lari, *Seal of the Prophets and His Message: Lessons on Islamic Doctrine*, trans. Hamid Algar (Potomac, Md.: Islamic Education Center, n.d.),

⟨http://www.al-islam.org/Seal/⟩.

7. Jalal al-Din Davani, *Akhlaq-i Jalali* (Lahore: Taj Book Depot, n.d.), chap. 5, p. 260.

8. For mystical concepts of Muhammad, see Carl W. Ernst, *Shambhala Guide to Sufism* (Boston: Shambhala Publications, 1997), chap. 2, and Carl W. Ernst, *Teachings of Sufism* (Boston: Shambhala Publications, 1999), chap. 2.

9. An excellent resource in this respect is the superb translation by Michael Sells, *Approaching the Qur'an: The Early Revelations* (Ashland, Ore.: White Cloud Press, 1999), which contains a CD-ROM with recordings of recitations of the Qur'an by a variety of reciters. A useful website with the Arabic text and audio recordings of Qur'anic recitation is available at ‹http://islamicity.com/mosque/ArabicScript/sindex.htm›. For complete versions of the Qur'an, see the translations of A. J. Arberry, *The Koran Interpreted* (New York: Macmillan, 1955); Ahmed Ali, *al-Qur'an: A Contemporary Translation* (Princeton: Princeton University Press, 1988).

10. Bart D. Ehrman, *The Orthodox Corruption of Scripture: The Effect of Early Christological Controversies on the Text of the New Testament* (Oxford: Oxford University Press, 1996).

11. It is said, for instance, that the manuscript of Ibn Mas'ud contained an interesting variant on Qur'an 3:19, "religion (or service), with God, is submission *(islam)*"; the last word in his copy was *hanifiyya*, the generic term for monotheism ("al-Kur'an," *Encyclopaedia of Islam* [Leiden: E. J. Brill, 1960–], 5:400a).

12. Toby Lester, "What Is the Koran?," *Atlantic Monthly*, January 1999; an online version is available at
‹http://www.theatlantic.com/issues/99jan/koran.htm›.

13. Kenneth L. Woodward, "In the Beginning, There Were the Holy Books," *Newsweek*, February 11, 2002; the article is available online at ‹http://www.bintjbeil.com/articles/en/020211_islam.html› (February 28, 2003).

14. Rosalind Gwynne, "Al-Qa'ida and al-Qur'an: The 'Tafsir' [Commentary] of Usamah bin Ladin," unpublished paper available online at ‹http://web.utk.edu/~warda/bin_ladin_and_quran.htm›.

15. For an example of Sufi meditation on the Qur'an, see Ernst, *Teachings of Sufism*, chap. 1, pp. 1–14.

Chapter Four

Arabic epigraph: A famous hadith of the Prophet Muhammad: "Anoint yourself with the character of God." The term "character" (*akhlaq*) is also the standard Arabic translation for "ethics" in philosophical texts.

1. For a detailed Shi'i justification of the use of the clay pillow from Kerbela, see ‹http://www.al-islam.org/beliefs/practices/turba.htm›.

2. Bernard G. Weiss, *The Spirit of Islamic Law* (Athens: University of Georgia Press, 1988).

3. Muhammad ibn 'Abd Allah al-Tabrizi, *Mishkat al-masabih* (New Delhi: al-Maktaba al-Rashidiyya, 1955), Bab al-Imara, p. 319; Bab al-Kasb, p. 241; Bab al-Jihad, p. 331. For a translation, see James Robson, trans., *Mishkat al-Masabih* (Lahore: S. M. Ashraf, 1963–65).

4. In the 1980s in California, someone protested against an automobile vanity license plate that read "JIHAD." It was alleged that the word "jihad" was an incitement to violence. It turned out that the license plate belonged to a teenage boy whose name was Jihad; his Arab-American parents had named him after a supreme virtue, struggle for truth.

5. See Carl W. Ernst, *Eternal Garden: Mysticism, History, and Politics at a South Asian Sufi Center* (Albany: State University of New York Press, 1992), esp. 29–37.

6. Muzaffar Alam, "Sharia and Governance in Indo-Islamic Context," in *Beyond Turk and Hindu: Rethinking Religious Identities in Islamicate South Asia*, ed. David Gilmartin and Bruce B. Lawrence (Gainesville: University Press of Florida, 2000).

7. Jalal al-Din Davani, *Akhlaq-i Jalali* (Lahore: Taj Book Depot, n.d.), 287–88.

8. Henry Corbin, *The Voyage and the Messenger: Iran and Philosophy*, trans. Joseph H. Rowe (Berkeley, Calif.: North Atlantic Books, 1998). For a website with detailed information on Islamic philosophy, see ‹http://www.muslimphilosophy.com/›.

9. Amira El Azhary Sonbol, ed., *Women, the Family, and Divorce Laws in Islamic History*, Contemporary Issues in the Middle East (Syracuse, N.Y.: Syracuse University Press, 1996).

10. For an illuminating treatment of Islam in politics by national context, see Bruce B. Lawrence, *Shattering the Myth: Islam beyond Violence* (Princeton: Princeton University Press, 2000).

11. For an online version of the Constitution of Iran, see
‹http://www.uni-wuerzburg.de/law/ir__indx.html›.

12. See Charles Kurzman, ed., *Liberal Islam: A Source-Book* (Oxford: Oxford University Press, 1998); this is an anthology containing writings by thirty-two different twentieth-century Muslims on the subjects of democracy, women's rights, freedom of thought, and progress. For Internet resources on liberal Islam, see
‹http://www.unc.edu/~kurzman/LiberalIslamLinks.htm›.

13. Azim Nanji, "Islamic Ethics," in *A Companion to Ethics*, ed. Peter Singer (Oxford: Blackwells, 1991), 106–18; an online version is available at
‹http://www.iis.ac.uk/learning/life_long_learning/islamic_ethics/
islamic_ethics.htm›.

14. Richard C. Martin and Mark R. Woodward, with Dwi S. Atmaja, *Defenders of Reason in Islam: Mu'tazilism from Medieval School to Modern Symbol* (Oxford: Oneworld, 1997). See also Farid Esack, *Qur'an, Liberation, and Pluralism* (Oxford: Oneworld, 1997).

15. Abdul-Karim Soroush, "The Evolution and Devolution of Religious Knowledge," in Kurzman, *Liberal Islam*, 246. For a website devoted to the thought of this philosopher, see ‹http://www.seraj.org›.

16. M. H. Bilgrami, *The Victory of Truth: The Life of Zaynab bint 'Ali* (Karachi: Zahra Publications Pakistan, 1986); an online version is available at ‹http://www.al-islam.org/victory/›.

17. For a cogent and persuasive discussion of these issues, see Leila Ahmed, *Women and Gender in Islam: Historical Roots of a Modern Debate* (New Haven: Yale University Press, 1992), esp. 144–55.

18. Ibid., 41–63.

19. Nazira Zayn al-Din, in Kurzman, *Liberal Islam*. See also miriam cooke, *Women Claim Islam: Creating Islamic Feminism through Literature* (New York: Routledge, 2001).

20. Fatima Mernissi, *The Veil and the Male Elite: A Feminist Interpretation of Women's Rights in Islam* (Cambridge: Perseus Books, 1987).

21. See the Islamic Family Law website
(‹http://els41.law.emory.edu/ifl/›),
which contains extensive documentation about the status of Islamic law and its implementation in different countries around the world.

22. Ziba Mir-Hosseini, *Islam and Gender: The Religious Debate in Contemporary Iran* (Princeton: Princeton University Press, 1999). See also

the film *Divorce Iranian Style*, directed by Kim Longinotto and Ziba Mir-Hosseini, which describes how women negotiate their way through the Iranian judicial system (available from Women Make Movies, at
⟨http://www.wmm.com/Catalog/pages/c454.htm⟩).

23. Maria Jaschok and Shui Jinjun, *The History of Women's Mosques in Chinese Islam* (Surrey: Curzon Press, 2000).

24. Seyyed Hossein Nasr, *Science and Civilization in Islam*, 2nd ed. (Cambridge: Islamic Texts Society, 1987).

25. David A. King, *Astronomy in the Service of Islam* (Brookfield, Vt.: Variorum, 1993).

26. Imperial decree of the mother of Ottoman Emperor Suleiman Qanuni ("the Magnificent"), trans. Dr. F. Canguzel Zulfikar.

27. Fazlur Rahman, *Health and Medicine in the Islamic Tradition: Change and Identity* (New York: Crossroad, 1987).

28. Bernard Lewis, *What Went Wrong? Western Impact and Middle Eastern Response* (Oxford: Oxford University Press, 2001).

29. For an important critical review of Lewis's book by a respected historian, see Juan Cole, in *Global Dialogue* 4, no. 4 (Autumn 2002) (available online at ⟨http://electronicIntifada.net/v2/article1121.shtml⟩).

30. George Saliba, "Whose Science Is Arabic Science in Renaissance Europe?," available online at
⟨http://www.columbia.edu/~gas1/project/visions/case1/sci.1.html⟩;
Mohamad Tavakoli-Targhi, *Refashioning Iran: Orientalism, Occidentalism, and Historiography* (New York: Palgrave, 2001); J. Knappert, "Nudjum," *Encyclopaedia of Islam* (Leiden: E. J. Brill, 1960–), 8:97–105.

31. Tavakoli-Targhi, *Refashioning Iran*, chap. 1 (available online at
⟨http://www.history.ilstu.edu/mtavakol/refashion.pdf⟩).

32. See the selections by al-Farabi, Ibn Sina, and Ibn Rushd in *Medieval Political Philosophy: A Sourcebook*, ed. Ralph Lerner and Muhsin Mahdi (New York: Free Press of Glencoe, 1963).

33. One of the earliest efforts of this kind was the 1867 work by the North African scholar Khayr al-Din al-Tunisi, *The Surest Path: The Political Treatise of a Nineteenth-Century Muslim Statesman*, trans. and ed. Leon Carl Brown (Cambridge: Harvard Middle East Monograph Series, 1967).

34. Leif Stenberg, *The Islamization of Science: Four Muslim Positions Developing an Islamic Modernity* (Lund, Sweden: Lund University, 1996).

35. Maurice Bucaille, *The Bible, the Qur'an, and Science: The Holy*

Scriptures Examined in the Light of Modern Knowledge (Chicago: Kazi Publications, 1989).

36. Pervez Hoodbhoy, *Islam and Science: Religious Orthodoxy and the Battle for Rationality* (London: Zed Books, 1991).

Chapter Five

Arabic epigraph: From an important Qur'anic passage (10:62): "The friends of God—for them there is no fear, neither do they grieve." This is commonly understood as referring to the saints, those who are closest to God and help others approach God.

1. William James, *The Varieties of Religious Experience: A Study in Human Nature, Being the Gifford lectures on natural religion delivered at Edinburgh in 1901–1902* (London: Longmans, Green, 1906; reprint, Cambridge: Harvard University Press, 1985).

2. Carl W. Ernst, "From Philosophy of Religion to History of Religion," in *Problems in the Philosophy of Religion: Critical Studies of the Work of John Hick*, ed. Harold Hewitt Jr. (London: Macmillan, 1991), 46–50.

3. Pseudo-Dionysius, *The Complete Works*, trans. Colm Luibheid, Classics of Western Spirituality (Mahwah, N.J.: Paulist Press, 1988). For a comprehensive overview of Christian mysticism, see the multivolume series by Bernard McGinn, *Presence of God: A History of Western Christian Mysticism* (New York: Crossroad, 1994–2001).

4. Annemarie Schimmel, *Mystical Dimensions of Islam* (Chapel Hill: University of North Carolina Press, 1975).

5. For a recent translation, see Jalal al-Din Rumi, *The Soul of Rumi: A New Collection of Ecstatic Poems*, trans. Coleman Barks (San Francisco: Harper San Francisco, 2001). An excellent comprehensive biography of Rumi is Franklin Lewis, *Rumi: Past and Present, East and West* (London: Oneworld, 2001).

6. See Carl W. Ernst, *Shambhala Guide to Sufism* (Boston: Shambhala Publications, 1997), which treats many of the subjects touched upon in this chapter in considerably more detail.

7. Although some readers may be more familiar with the term "Shi'ites," that form of the name is archaic and reminds one of the Amelikites and Moabites of the Bible. It is preferable to use the term "Shi'i" for a member of this group, and "Shi'a" for the group itself, since this is how the terms are used in Arabic and Persian.

8. For comprehensive information on the Isma'ili tradition, see the website of the Institute of Isma'ili Studies

(‹http://www.iis.ac.uk/home_l1.htm›).

See also Farhad Daftary, *The Ismailis: Their History and Doctrines* (Cambridge: Cambridge University Press, 1990).

9. For information on the Dawoodi Bohras, see

‹http://www.mumineen.org/›.

A recent study is Jonah Blank, *Mullahs on the Mainframe: Islam and Modernity among the Daudi Bohras* (Chicago: University of Chicago Press, 2001).

10. An extensive online collection of early Shi'i authoritative texts and multimedia resources has been assembled by the Ahlul Bayt Digital Islam Library Project (‹http://www.al-islam.org/organizations/dilp/›).

11. Mohammad Ali Amir-Moezzi and Jean Calmard, "Fatima," in *Encyclopaedia Iranica* (Costa Mesa, Calif.: Mazda Publishers, 1999).

12. Mohammad Ali Amir-Moezzi, *The Divine Guide in Early Shi'ism: The Sources of Esotericism in Islam*, trans. David Streight (Albany: State University of New York Press, 1994).

13. David Pinault, *The Shiites: Ritual and Popular Piety in a Muslim Community* (New York: Palgrave, 1993).

14. Peter Chelkowski, *Ta'ziyeh: Ritual and Drama in Iran* (New York: New York University Press, 1979).

15. The office of Iran's supreme leader, Ayatollah Khamenei, has an official website at ‹http://www.wilayah.org/english/default.htm›.

16. For a classic account of pilgrimage to Kerbela by an American anthropologist, see Elizabeth Warnock Fernea, *Guests of the Sheik: An Ethnography of an Iraqi Village* (New York: Anchor Books, 1969; reprint, 1989).

17. Striking pictures of the shrines at Medina before and after the 1925 demolition may be seen at

‹http://www.al-islam.org/gallery/photos/image2nd.htm›.

18. *'Umar Ibn Al-Farid: Sufi Verse, Saintly Life*, trans. Th. Emil Homerin, Classics of Western Spirituality (Mahwah, N.J.: Paulist Press, 2001).

19. Regula Burckhardt Qureshi, *Sufi Music of India and Pakistan: Sound, Context, and Meaning in Qawwali* (Chicago: University of Chicago Press, 1995), with audio CD.

20. Shems Friedlander, *The Whirling Dervishes: Being an Account of the*

Sufi Order Known as the Mevlevis and Its Founder the Poet and Mystic Mevlana Jalalu'ddin Rumi (Albany: State University of New York Press, 1991).

21. For an example of this North African/Andalusian music, see Maroc/Ustad Massano Tazi, *Musique classique andalouse de Fes,* OCORA Radio France, C559035.

22. Extensive information on the Mouridiyya and Islam in Senegal is found on the website of Yale graduate student J. Ben Hill
(‹http://www.geocities.com/jbenhill/religion.html›).
The "Passport to Paradise" exhibit of Mouride art at UCLA is documented at ‹http://www.fmch.ucla.edu/paradise/main001.htm›.

23. For discographies of Sufi music recordings, see Ernst, *Guide to Sufism,* and "The Selflessly Sacred Art of Whooping It Up," *Spirituality and Health,* Spring 2002, 55.

24. For a sensitive and comprehensive introduction to Islamic spirituality and art in the broadest sense, see two books by John Renard, *Seven Doors to the House of Islam: Spirituality and the Religious Life of Muslims* (Berkeley: University of California Press, 1996) and *Windows on the House of Islam: Muslim Sources on Spirituality and Religious Life* (Berkeley: University of California Press, 1998).

25. Jonathan Bloom and Sheila Blair, *Islamic Arts* (London: Phaidon Press, 1997), 1, introduction.

26. For a list of basic reference works on Islamic art and links to major museum collections, see the Islamic Art and Architecture web page at the Sloane Art Library at the University of North Carolina at Chapel Hill (‹http://www.lib.unc.edu/art/islamicart.html›).

27. For extensive visual and textual resources on Islamic architecture, see the ArchNet website at the MIT School of Architecture and Planning (‹http://archnet.org/lobby.tcl›).

28. Renard, *Seven Doors,* 44–48.

29. For contemporary examples of Islamic architectural ornamentation, see ‹http://www.Bonner-design.com/index.htm›.

30. Carl W. Ernst, "The Spirit of Islamic Calligraphy: Baba Shah Isfahani's *Adab al-mashq," Journal of the American Oriental Society* 112 (1992): 279–86 (‹http://www.unc.edu/courses/relio60a/BABASHAH.htm›). For examples, see Mamoun Sakkal, "The Art of Arabic Calligraphy"
(‹http://www.sakkal.com/ArtArabicCalligraphy.html›).

31. Carl W. Ernst, *Eternal Garden: Mysticism, History, and Politics at a South Asian Sufi Center* (Albany: State University of New York Press, 1992), 32–33.

32. Ciclo Internacional de Exposiciones Museo Sin Fronteras, *El Arte Mudéjar: La estética islámica en el arte cristiano* (Vienna: Electa, 2000); English translation, *Spain: Mudejar Art—Islamic Aesthetics in Christian Art* (London: Art Book International, 2002).

33. Jean-Baptiste Vanmour, *One Hundred Prints Representing Different Nations of the Levant* (Paris, 1712–13), quoted by Lisa Small, "Western Eyes, Eastern Visions," in *A Distant Muse: An Orientalist Works from the Dahesh Museum of Art* (New York: Dahesh Museum of Art, 2000), 9.

34. Leslie P. Pierce, *The Imperial Harem: Women and Sovereignty in the Ottoman Empire*, Studies in Middle Eastern History (Oxford: Oxford University Press, 1993).

35. Holly Edwards, *Noble Dreams, Wicked Pleasures: Orientalism in America, 1870–1930* (Princeton: Princeton University Press, 2000); ‹http://www.tfaoi.com/aa/1aa/1aa506.htm›.

36. For a documentary on images of Middle Eastern women in American films, see *Hollywood Harems*, produced and written by Tania Kamal-Eldin (Women Make Movies, 1999, ‹http://www.wmm.com/catalog/pages/c482.htm›); see also Jack G. Shaheen, *Reel Bad Arabs: How Hollywood Vilifies a People* (Northampton, Mass.: Interlink Publishing Group, 2001).

37. For these observations, I draw on Judith Ernst, "The Problem of Islamic Art," in *Muslim Networks: Medium, Method, and Metaphor*, ed. miriam cooke and Bruce B. Lawrence, Islamic Civilization and Muslim Networks (Chapel Hill: University of North Carolina Press, forthcoming).

38. Layla S. Diba, Maryam Ekhtiar, and B. W. Robinson, eds., *Royal Persian Paintings: The Qajar Epoch, 1785–1925* (London: I. B. Tauris, 1998).

39. *Manifestation of Feeling: A Selection of Painting by Iranian Female Artists* (Tehran: Center for Visual Arts, Ministry of Culture and Islamic Guidance, 1995).

40. Judith Ernst, "Problem of Islamic Art," 7–8.

41. Michael A. Sells, "Erasing Culture: Wahhabism, Buddhism, Balkan Mosques" (‹http://www.haverford.edu/relg/sells/reports/WahhabismBuddhasBegova.htm›).

Chapter Six

Arabic epigraph: From a famous hadith of the Prophet Muhammad: "Difference of opinion in my community is a mercy."

1. Stephen Hay, *Asian Ideas of East and West: Tagore and His Critics in Japan, China, and India* (Cambridge: Harvard University Press, 1970).

2. For a study of religion and violence around the world today, see Mark Juergensmeyer, *Terror in the Mind of God* (Berkeley: University of California Press, 2000).

3. For a summary of this case, see
‹http://www.soas.ac.uk/Centres/IslamicLaw/YB1Zaheer-ud-din.html›.

4. Remarkably, it is the commodity of Coca-Cola that serves as a symbol of globalization for Muslim boycott movements protesting U.S. foreign policy. Iran's entry into this field was Zamzam Cola (named after the sacred fountain in Mecca), while a French citizen of Tunisian background introduced Mecca-Cola for the same purpose early in 2003.

5. For a list of suggested novels from Muslim majority countries, see
‹http://www.unc.edu/~cernst/novels.htm›.

6. Gary R. Bunt, *Virtually Islamic: Computer-Mediated Communication and Cyber Islamic Environments* (Cardiff: University of Wales Press, 2000).

SUGGESTED FURTHER READING

Basic Sources

Armstrong, Karen. *Muhammad: A Biography of the Prophet*. San Francisco: Harper San Francisco, 1993.

Schimmel, Annemarie. *And Muhammad Is His Messenger: The Veneration of the Prophet in Islamic Piety*. Chapel Hill: University of North Carolina Press, 1985.

Sells, Michael. *Approaching the Qur'an: The Early Revelations* (with audio CD). Ashland, Ore.: White Cloud Press, 1999.

Weiss, Bernard G. *The Spirit of Islamic Law*. Athens: University of Georgia Press, 1988.

Gender Issues

Ahmed, Leila. *Women and Gender in Islam: Historical Roots of a Modern Debate*. New Haven: Yale University Press, 1992.

cooke, miriam. *Women Claim Islam: Creating Islamic Feminism through Literature*. New York: Routledge, 2001.

Mernissi, Fatima. *The Veil and the Male Elite: A Feminist Interpretation of Women's Rights in Islam*. Translated by Mary Jo Lakeland. Cambridge: Perseus Books, 1987.

Islam in the Modern World

Bunt, Gary R. *Virtually Islamic: Computer-Mediated Communication and Cyber Islamic Environments*. Cardiff: University of Wales Press, 2000.

Eickelman, Dale F., and James Piscatori. *Muslim Politics*. Princeton: Princeton University Press, 1996.

Kurzman, Charles, ed. *Liberal Islam: A Sourcebook*. Oxford: Oxford University Press, 1998.

Lawrence, Bruce B. *Shattering the Myth: Islam beyond Violence.*
Princeton: Princeton University Press, 2000.

Safi, Omid, ed. *Progressive Muslims on Gender, Justice, and Pluralism.*
Oxford: Oneworld, 2003.

Spirituality and Art

Amir-Moezzi, Mohammad Ali. *The Divine Guide in Early Shi'ism: The
Sources of Esotericism in Islam.* Translated by David Streight. Albany:
State University of New York Press, 1994.

Bloom, Jonathan, and Sheila Blair. *Islamic Arts.* London: Phaidon Press
Limited, 1997.

Ernst, Carl W. *The Shambhala Guide to Sufism.* Boston: Shambhala
Publications, 1997.

————. *Teachings of Sufism.* Boston: Shambhala Publications, 1999.

INDEX

159, 191; defined as universal, 212. *See also* East; Science: Islamization of

Civilizations: dialogue of, 3, 141, 209; clash of, 3, 215 (n. 3)

Clothing, in different Muslim countries, 146–48, 192. *See also* Veiling

Coca-Cola, 205, 229 (n. 4)

Colonialism, 18, 28–29, 40, 48, 118, 121, 133, 140, 200; and military superiority, 7, 20; and Eurocentrism, 8, 124, 139; and Islamic law, 104; justifications for, 144, 151, 158. *See also* Americans; Britain; France; Military technology; Russians; Soviets

Columbian Exposition of 1898, 193

Comte, Auguste, 20

Confucianism, 59

Constitutions, 31, 57; Iranian, 138–39

Conversion: of Muslims and Jews to Christianity, 17; to Islam, 61, 90, 120

Copernicus, 157

Corbin, Henry, 126

Courts, 57, 205

Creationists, 161

Cromer, Lord, 144

Crusades, 6–7, 101

Curzon, Lord, 144

Custom, pre-Islamic, 31, 47, 104, 110, 116, 150–51

Dalai Lama, 11

Damascus, 142, 186

Dante, 16

Darwinism, 160–61

Davani, Jalal al-Din, 83–84, 121–24, 136

David, 45

Delhi, 153, 188

Della Valle, Pietro, 157

Democracy, 34, 140, 208, 212

Deoband, 129–31

Descartes, René, 127, 157

Deuteronomy, 33

Devil, 22, 98

Din (religion, duty), 65

Dionysius, 165

Dome of the Rock, 87, 100, 186

Druze, 170

East: as spiritual opposite of Europe, 23, 190–94, 201, 208; geographic meaning of, 202

East Africa, 170

East India Company, 157

Eckhard, Meister, 165

Education, 128–29, 140

Egypt, 60, 128, 133, 134, 146, 148, 149, 180, 191

Eidhi Foundation, 135

Embryology, 159

Empire, 208; Ottoman, 6, 17, 20, 26, 28, 66, 131–33, 153, 190, 191, 192; Roman, 6, 47, 85, 89, 90, 115, 120, 146; Persian, 47, 85, 90, 120, 121, 146, 156; Arab, 90, 117, 119–20, 146; Mughal, 128, 153, 188; Safavid, 179; Byzantine, 186

Engels, Friedrich, 20

Engineers, 161

Enlightenment, 20, 34, 43, 140